THE HIGSON HOME BUYER'S GUIDE

ALSO BY JAMES D. HIGSON:

The Higson Home-Builder's Guide

THE HIGSON HOME BUYER'S GUIDE

JAMES D. HIGSON

ILLUSTRATED BY PEGGY LYNCH

Nash Publishing
Los Angeles

Library of Congress Catalog Card Number: 72-95247
International Standard Book Number: 0-8402-1292-5

Published simultaneously in the United States and Canada
by Nash Publishing Corporation, 9255 Sunset Boulevard,
Los Angeles, California 90069.

Printed in the United States of America.

First Printing.

For my father, who remembers
and enjoyed all of the houses.

CONTENTS

PREFACE

If you were to observe anyone paying some thousands of dollars for an oil painting, a Renaissance chest, a Stradivarius violin or, for that matter, seventy-five dollars for a bottle of 1961 Chateau Lafite Rothschild, you would assume that the person had a considerable fund of knowledge in the respective field of art, antiques, violins or wines, and you would undoubtedly be right. Unless one were a wastrel or a simpleton, one would rarely make a financial commitment of this type without the broad, basic historical and technical marketing knowledge that would enable him to be confident that his decision is sound.

It is all the more wonder, then, that each year thousands of people continue to buy new homes with little more care and discretion than they would use in buying a new car or, in some cases, even a new hat. America is the most mobile civilization in history—20 percent of the population changes residences every year. The new house is, in the vast majority of cases, the most expensive purchase the person will ever make, often involving the savings of a lifetime. It is, as well, fundamental to the day-to-day happiness of one's entire family.

As important a decision as it is, we all nonetheless can easily recall endless examples of people having bought their homes after they've rushed about for a few days and viewed perhaps only a half-dozen properties. If the end result is an acquisition that was overpriced, in poor repair and unsuitable to the buyer's needs, one can hardly be surprised. Erring in buying a house is no joke. One can laugh at having splurged on an article of clothing which has never been out of the closet, but to be stuck with a house in which you are unhappy, and one which you are unable to resell, is no laughing matter.

The prospective home buyer should approach the task with some critical judgment, some means of comparison, some standards of measurement in the many phases of house evaluation. Otherwise, he will only be able to act out of intuition, emotion and the pressures of the moment. It is this book's intent, therefore, to broaden the buyer's horizons in many respects and also to establish some priorities within these broadened horizons. Beyond the basic fundamental facts of house buying, I have tried to alert you to various observations that should be made, questions that should be asked. With the use of these guidelines, plus a sufficient exercise of time and reason on the buyer's part, there is no reason why you should not acquire a home that you will enjoy for years—as well as one that is a sound investment.

One thing to bear in mind is that in some respects the seller always has the advantage. If he is the owner of the property he will know about deficiencies which he can hide (a crate over the sump pump in the basement, concealing from you the fact that the basement leaks and a sump pump is necessary), or if he can't hide them he can distract you from noticing them by various other wiles: bouquets of flowers burgeoning from every table, stereo music playing throughout the house, the aroma of an apple pie cooking in the oven. You will remember the old nursery rhyme, " 'Will you walk into my parlor?' said the spider to the fly . . ."; whereupon the spider "wove a subtle web." Always remember that *you* are the fly.

Further, the craftiest of individual home owners is but a rank amateur in comparison to the large firms marketing tracts of residential housing. With their research people and marketing experts working full time, they probably know more about you than you do yourself. And, as in the case of Pavlov's dog, they know just which bells to ring to make you salivate automatically. Their "models" are professionally decorated at great expense and lavishly landscaped. They employ experts in marketing to maximize their sales presentation, experts in production to keep costs low while still providing or appearing to provide a salable product, and experts in finance to blunt the severity and enormity of the commitment by the tailoring of that form of indenture, the long-term mortgage or deed of trust. Overall, the large merchandisers of homes have done their homework and mounted a professional job of marketing their product. This expertise has even disseminated itself to the general real estate trade via the forums where used houses are resold and where new speculative houses, called "spec" houses, are offered on an individual basis.

It must be clear to the prospective buyer that he should arm himself with as much applicable information on the product he is shopping for *prior* to his exposure to the wiles of a real estate salesman or the temptation of the home product itself. Moreover, he should attempt to develop some sense of order in applying this knowledge, since some parts of it will rank higher than others in helping create a well-ordered decision.

This will be the point in the ensuing pages. Since the dawn of commerce, the Latin phrase *caveat emptor* (meaning literally, "let the buyer beware") has lost none of its force, and for good reason.

THE HIGSON HOME BUYER'S GUIDE

1
WHY NOT RENT?

Sylvia Porter, the financial columnist, has stated that the single and early married years from 22 to 30 are best suited to renting an apartment. Why not continue this pattern on into your mid 30s or into your 40s? Let us analyze the attractiveness of continuing to rent.

The Cost of Shelter

You should plan not to spend more than 25 percent of your gross income for shelter.

Therefore, if the combined gross income of husband and wife totals $16,000, their allocation for rent *or* home ownership and maintenance should not exceed $330 a month. If you rent an apartment, condominium or house, you can apply the entire amount as rent. If you plan to buy a condominium or house, this money for shelter must be split between the major house-mortgage payment and a group of extra expenses like taxes, insurance, utilities and repairs.

How to Compare Renting with Buying

Take the shelter figure used above ($330 a month) and make the following comparison:

Cost to Rent		*Cost to Buy a $42,000 House* *	
Rent	$330	Mortgage payments (principal and interest on $35,000 loan)	$250
		Taxes (1/10)	33
		Insurance (1/20)	17
		Utilities	10
		Repairs	20
Total Cost to Rent	$330	Total Cost to Buy	$330

Advantages of Renting

Shorter-Term Commitment.

A landlord renting you an apartment or home is willing to sign a lease for a year with rights for you to renew. When you buy a home or condominium, you can only get out of your commitment by reselling it, which can sometimes be a lengthy process.

---

*This house cost is based on the old maxim, "Buy a house that costs 2-1/2 times your annual income." These days, you will be hard put to find something suitable for less than three times your annual income.

Preservation of Capital.

Renting does not require a down payment. You only have to pay the first and last month's rent, plus whatever cleaning and breakage deposit is required. Thus, the rest of your capital is free for other purposes.

Freedom from Maintenance.

Your landlord has the responsibility for repairs and maintenance of rental properties. You can come and go as you please without the cares of management. Most condominiums, however, have some kind of management that could leave you about as free from these concerns as apartment units do.

Slightly Less Expensive in the Short Term.

The type of "shelter money" comparison shown above often favors renting over buying, because it is unable to incorporate the factors of appreciation and tax advantages. So in a short-term analysis of the relative costs, you can expect the rental side to show up more favorably if the properties are comparable.

Advantages of Buying

Land Value Appreciation.

If your condominium or home is wisely selected as to location, there will be an enhancement of the value of the bare land on which the improvements are built. It is possible *only* through ownership to participate in this rise in value. George Washington once wrote, "The best investment on earth is earth."

Appreciation Due to Spiraling Building Costs.

The cost of building goes up between 7 and 8 percent a year. The well-built condominium or home of today should not depreciate. Instead, it may very well increase in value when it is compared with structures of lesser quality and higher cost in years to come.

Improvement during Ownership.

Some improvements in a property can only come about through time. Your trees, hedges, shrubbery and lawn will mature and, presumably, prosper. Also, as a conscientious owner you can invest many hours in planning and work on landscaping and improvements that will buttress the value of the property.

Hedge against Inflation.

If you expect the inflationary movement to continue, and almost everybody does, a property well bought today will simply be worth more money in years to come. Obviously, in a rental you have no way that you can ride along on this increase. You will merely be paying more and more rent and not *pinning down* the cost of your investment initially and watching its value grow as the dollar's value erodes.

Tax Advantages.

The interest on your mortgage note is deductible, along with your property taxes. If you sell the property for a gain, you will not have to pay any tax on the gain if you reinvest at least the amount of the sales price in another property within a year, or within eighteen months if you build.

Pride of Ownership.

Pride of ownership is still the major motivating force in buying a home. Though contemporary Americans rarely think of the family homestead as something to be passed on from generation to generation, the overriding compulsion toward territorial enfranchisement and its concomitant trait of nest building are too strong for most of us to withstand. The home is not only the possession most critical to everyday enjoyment, it is as well the possession by which you will probably be most judged by your friends and the community. Like it or not, even true or not, people assume that a person's house reflects his taste, life-style, affluence, etc. Indeed, it has been said that the house in its deepest essence is a projection of the ego. So, you cannot deny the nest-building trait in animal and man, and this desire for permanence is a frequent tie-breaker in the rent-or-buy argument. You can plant your feet in your condo or home in the knowledge that part of the funds spent for shelter are creating a lasting and growing investment.

Singles as Buyers

As an outgrowth of the "swinging singles" apartment development, the idea of condominium ownership by single individuals has evolved. There is no reason why singles and young marrieds should not share in the advantages of equity buildup as freely as older families. If they have a decent income, mortgage lenders accept them as readily as anyone else. The condominium setup is more appealing to singles because of the lack of maintenance and responsibility, but the principles of investment are just as applicable for them.

WHY NOT BUILD? 2

The Arguments for Building

The Creative Urge.

Nest building is a basic trait evident in all living things around us. There lies within most of us a desire to build our own nest, our home, our castle. It is not that an existing house could not satisfy our minimal requirements, or that a building company could not build us an adequate shelter. You just feel compelled to build your own individual home.

Previous Ownership of Lot.

You may be involved in some property that for one reason or another needs developing in order to provide you shelter. You might be planning to divide the lot you presently live on, or perhaps you have inherited a site or have acquired one by some means that at this current stage of planning looks as if it would provide a good location for a home.

Building to Obtain an Area You Want.

Sometimes you have to tear down an existing old house or acquire a lot that has been around for a long time in order to

9

secure a particular neighborhood location you desire. Also, in undeveloped areas there is little market to attract tract or "spec" builders, and there is often no alternative to building your own home.

The Hazards of Building

Temperament.

In the preface to *The Higson Home-Builder's Guide,* we state that some people are constitutionally incapable of building a home. Sometimes it is the disposition of the man of the family which will preclude home building. He may be too tense with office problems, personal worries or money pressures. Sometimes the woman of the household has difficulty making decisions and dreads a yearlong project where decisions are necessary to the progress of the house. More generally, there exists a sort of common tension whereby cooperation is difficult.

Saint Exupéry has said that love is not looking at each other but looking in the same direction. Whether you agree with this sentiment or not, home building demands a lot of looking in the same direction. If you are not prepared to make the commitment in emotion and time that the project entails, do not try to construct you own home. You will not only make yourself and family miserable, but you will affect dozens of other people for months into the future.

Length of Construction Time.

Most houses take from six to nine months to build. Then when you add to this period the design work, the bidding of the contract, the final landscaping, cleaning, carpeting, draping, plus actual moving in at the end, the normal gestation time works out to be more than a year. You will need to determine whether or not you can make this commitment of time. You simply may need to have possession of a home sooner than that.

What Is the Cost to Build?

Basic Construction of the House.

To start with, you must determine the correct square footage of the project. Add up all living spaces measured to the *outside* of the walls. We will take an example of a house of 2,000 square feet of living space.

Add about 2/3 of the footage area of the garage (in this case take 2/3 of 600 square feet, or 400 net square feet). Last, you will add 1/3 of any porches, balconies or large supported overhangs. The final count will look like this:

Living areas	2,000 square feet
Garage	400 square feet
Balconies, overhangs	300 square feet
Total net square footage	2,700 square feet

You are now ready to apply a cost-per-square-foot building figure to the net footage. In many areas of the country, this is currently around $20 a foot for a simple custom home. This would make the above example come out to $54,000. It goes without saying that you must add for a swimming pool, extensive landscaping, ambitious patios, extra fencing, etc. Therefore, our final building costs including extras and land might look like this:

Cost of land	$8,500
House plans	1,500
House construction	54,000
Swimming pool	4,500
Landscaping	2,400
Total house cost	$70,900

"Holding" Costs.

Do not overlook another very real cost of building—the "holding" costs. This is the cost of owning the lot during the period of construction, and the cost of money applied to the house during construction. If you arranged a loan of $50,000 for the construction of the house, there would still be an additional $20,900 of cash going into the $70,900 project, including the original cost of the lot, plus some extra cash required for construction:

Cost of house and lot		$70,900
Interest lost on cash invested in lot		
(5-1/2% x 10 months)	390	
Interest lost on cash invested in house		
(over and above loan)	570	
Total interest lost		960
Real estate taxes pro-rata 10 months		1,740
Cost of construction loan (3 points)		1,500
Interest on construction loan (9 months)		3,380
Move-in costs		430
Total cost of building house		$78,910

Financing Costs.

As indicated above, the financing costs on a new house to be constructed can be considerable. For one thing, 2 or 3 "points" are charged for such a new loan—this being the surcharge for the creation and administration of such a loan. For another, you are usually charged "Dutch interest," meaning that you pay interest on the *total* amount of the loan, even though the funds are not actually disbursed to you until various stages of progress are achieved in building the house.

By way of comparison, if you were taking over the loan on an existing house, the lender would usually charge 1/2 a point for transferring the loan to your name. Therefore, you can see the true analysis of the cost of a new home would likely run much higher than merely the cost of the house and lot together.

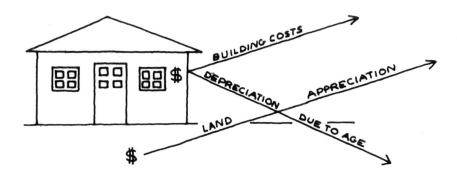

3
NEW VS. OLD

A new house for sale can either be a one-of-a-kind "speculative" house offered by a builder who speculates on single lots, or one of a tract or subdivision, usually sold from prototypes or "models." Old or used houses are simply houses that have had a previous owner, and they may in fact not be very old.

Location—Your Prime Consideration

There is an overriding consideration that should control your analysis of whether to buy a new or used house. It is location, location, *location!* A pursuit of the type of location that stands the most chance of appreciating over the years often tilts the scales in favor of the older home. The reason, of course, is that the choice, sought-after neighborhoods most often grow up in close proximity to the amenities, town centers, shops, schools, churches, recreational attractions and cultural assets of the city in which you are searching.

Few building sites remain in these established neighborhoods, and so it follows that the only way to achieve these choicer locations is to be content with a used house.

The task of selecting a site that will appreciate in a raw tract or subdivision is extremely tricky, but possible. You will want to consider factors such as minimum through traffic, house-to-lot orientation, recreational opportunities on the lot, overall setting, landscaping potentials and other items that might cause the property to excel over its neighbors and thus become a more marketable resale property.

In general, though, your best bet for sheer appreciation because of location is a good buy in a used home.

What about the Price?

There has been an 84 percent increase in housing costs since 1967, so used houses are generally cheaper to buy than new ones of equivalent square footage and quality. However, the story does not end there. You have to consider the added cost in a used house of refurbishing it to your requirements. Out-of-date appliances, poor bathrooms and inconvenient kitchens—to mention only a few of the most obvious areas of improvement—might satisfy you for the moment, but if you agree that these items have to be corrected, the cost of doing it is surely a cost to be added to the price of the house.

This is not to say that the new house is the complete answer either. It may have modern baths and kitchen and the latest models of appliances, but walls may be 1/2-inch drywall instead of inch-thick plaster, drains may be plastic instead of cast-iron, and doors may be hollow "slabs" instead of solid wood or paneled types. So, while reflecting a glossy, modern flash, the quality of construction may be inferior to the older, better-built home. It is up to you to make these distinctions. The ensuing chapters are filled with information designed to help you do this.

The Used-Home Dividends

Older buildings can also occasionally have enormous advantages in the sense of possessing features which have since been outlawed by building codes or zoning laws. A good example would be the older three-story house in an area where the maximum height limit is now 27 feet. Or the four-story townhouse which, if constructed now, would be required to have an elevator and a second set of stairs. Second kitchens and outside staircases are other features often not allowed these days in R-1 areas.

In looking at older homes, school yourself to look at the structure and the spaces and not at the worn carpeting and the mauve cabbage-rose wallpaper—things that can be changed at relatively little expense. Also steel yourself against dirt and bad housekeeping. A lot of potentially good buys are missed because the buyer cannot stomach the bad odors, the dirty dishes in the kitchen, the unmade beds or the douche bags hanging on bathroom doors.

Often in reselling an existing house, an owner more or less throws in appurtenances which are a very real cost in new construction. This applies to some free-standing appliances, to carpets, drapes, light fixtures, valances, and, in some cases, single-purpose furniture pieces such as an oversized dining table or bed, or built-in TV, hi-fi, etc., that he is willing to offer as "sweeteners."

Additionally, many older homes contain bookcases, cabinetry, light fixtures, hardware, wallpaper, mirrors, paneling, masonry, plumbing fixtures, marble, moldings, fireplace fittings far beyond the call of duty—and far beyond what you yourself might justify in creating a new-home plan, and far from what you would expect to see in a tract home. With building costs rising at about 7 to 8 percent a year, the obvious result has been a curtailment of these niceties that were previously taken for granted in even a modestly priced custom home.

Here is only a brief list of the kinds of items often found in older homes that have all but vanished from new spec or tract homes:

Extra bookcases	Garages longer than 20 feet
Cabinets other than kitchen and bath	Tile bathroom floors
	Hardwood *planked* floors

Wallpaper except baths and
  dressing room
Mirrored doors and walls
Paneling other than plywood
Masonry veneer
Elaborate plumbing fixtures
Shower sprays
Bidets
Formal fireplace marble surrounds
Herringbone firebrick
Any carving or mural work
Plaster molds and decorations
Rain gutters and downspouts
Dumbwaiters
Halls wider than 3 feet 6 inches
Pantries, vegetable coolers

Paneled doors
Heavy, cast doorknobs or levers
Rich door and window moldings
Cornices at ceiling edges
Bathtubs longer than 5 feet
Recirculating hot water
One-piece toilets
Wide-spread lavatory fittings
Large shower heads
Closets with operating locks
Ceilings higher than 8 feet
Window seats
Leaded glass windows
Clothes chutes
Back porches and mudrooms

Is Financing a Problem?

If the neighborhood is reasonably vital, there should be no difference in the financing obtainable between an older home and a new one. Sometimes, in tract financing, the builder has made an attractive contract with the overall lender on the total subdivision that enables you to get a maximum loan of, say, 80 percent of appraised value at fewer points and at less interest than you could obtain on the open market. This is certainly a plus value.

However, there is a strong likelihood that the older home you find will have financing on it already, and that the cost of increasing that will not be very much. As far as the maximum amount is concerned, most lenders like the buyer to have about 15 percent cash to put into the project (sometimes 10 percent), and often the seller of a used home will pick up the difference in the form of a second trust deed. Therefore, the possibility of an older home having attractive financing on it already, plus the chance that the seller would carry a second trust deed with reasonable terms, might nullify the attractiveness of the subdivider's loan arrangements.

4
HOME OR CONDOMINIUM?

The Fundamental Difference

In general, the difference between a home and a condominium is a matter of *density*—the density, that is, which the city or county involved will permit in a particular zoned area. Single-family residential lots must usually be a minimum of 6,000 square feet (60 by 100 feet in size), whereas condominium subdivisions usually permit a smaller amount of land use for each residential unit.

To obtain this type of high-density condominium subdivision, the developer usually proposes some common recreational or open spaces that can be used by all the owners collectively. This is why a condominium deed will include a legal description of the shelter area to be occupied by the owner, and an undivided interest in the common areas as well. You, as owner, will receive your tax bill based on this same description.

The Different Kinds of Condominiums

It is important to realize that size of structure does not have anything to do with whether it is a condominium or not. In some subdivisions, you can find condominiums as large as 3,000 or 3,500 square feet on their own plot of ground. Some communities call these *Planned Unit Developments* (P. U. D.), or *cluster housing,* but they are basically condominiums. At the other extreme, you will find a high-rise apartment building containing a hundred or more apartments. If these apartments can be purchased and a fee-simple title can be issued and insured, they are condominiums as well.

In general, though, the condominium concept signifies a higher-density use of land, a town-house or apartment style of living, and less of a sense of privacy than is found in a single-family dwelling. It is particularly suited to single people wishing to establish equities not available when renting an apartment, young marrieds for the same reason, older people wanting the security of a collective living arrangement, and those wanting housing in a resort area (usually a second home) where there is a management entity available to rent out empty condominiums and lighten this second home cost.

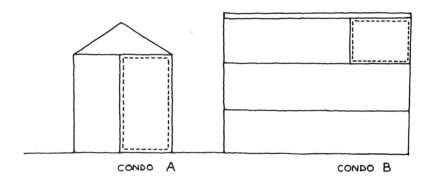

CONDO A   CONDO B

Town Houses—Either Condominium or Single Family

Sometimes called "row housing," this type of dwelling appears in all cities of the world that have been in existence for some time.

They are nothing more than narrow, multistory houses with little or no setbacks on the sides. They become condominiums when one or more units are created within the town houses and sold off separately. This is common practice in many large cities where it is not economically feasible for an investor to operate one of these buildings as an apartment house, but where he can add a reasonable profit on the sale of the units and ultimately dispose of the whole building to several buyers.

In the humorous vernacular used in larger cities, the fundamental width of one of these houses is indicated by the term "two-holer" or "three-holer"; once in a great while you might see a very narrow "one-holer." These nicknames refer to the amount of windows lining up on the street elevations.

TWO-HOLER   THREE-HOLER

The Single-Family Residence

The home that is separate from other houses ordinarily has the maximum of privacy, the maximum of land attached to the property, and, generally, the maximum opportunity for appreciation. As this book unfolds, we will be talking about the methods of improving the chances for this appreciation.

In Great Britain, the purchase of a home is considered to be the first truly important financial investment a person makes, when he is able. There is not even a contest between real estate and other investments that might be made. The building societies, as they are called there, stand ready to make an 80 to 90 percent loan on a property, in terms that are very reasonable, such as 25 to 30 years, at a low rate of interest and with low monthly payments.

In the United States, our savings and loans, both federal and state, and our large insurance companies are close behind England in offering an easy path to home ownership. If FHA financing is available, as it is on some homes, the buyer need only apply 10 percent to the purchase price of a house in order to arrange a 90 percent loan on the balance over a period of 30 years—and at a decent rate of interest.

In almost all other forms of consumer lending or personal finance, "add-on" interest is involved, whereby the *actual* rate paid is more like 14 to 18 percent. Residential housing loans remain one of the best "buys" in financing, since they call for interest to be paid *only* on the unpaid principal balance of the loan, and this balance is adjusted downward on a monthly basis as payments are made. Later on in our study, we will explore the intricacies of obtaining home financing.

5
WHERE TO LOOK
AND WHAT
TO LOOK FOR
IN ESTABLISHED
CITIES

Many of the criteria for house hunting in cities, subdivisions and out in the country are the same. Here we give emphasis to the points of greater significance in looking within the older, established city, its downtown area, neighborhoods and adjacent older suburbs.

The disadvantages of city living are easy to recite: polluted air, noise, antiquated housing and apartments, higher building and remodeling costs, less security, restricted outdoor areas and limited recreational pursuits. However, along with these faults, cities are the confluence of our civilized processes and products. The arts of music, the theater, drama, dance, painting, cinema and architecture are more readily available for study and enjoyment. Museums, libraries, bookshops, specialty stores and hundreds of unique services abound. Likewise, the hum of industry, commerce, science and education is a vital part of a medium-to-large city. Social life flourishes on all conceivable levels and in all varieties.

New home construction in the core of cities is extremely limited, but there is considerable activity in converting existing town houses and apartments into condominium units for sale.

When you combine this new vitality with the normal turnover of older homes for sale, you would do well to explore the heart of the city with imagination and industry. There are many reasons why the activity of the city can be quite appealing.

Before You Start Looking

Jack Nicklaus is renowned as a leading professional golfer, not an expert in the buying of homes. Yet in a recent lecture about preparing to address the golf ball, he gave a peculiar and fascinating instruction. "Look around you," he said. "Do this first before anything else."

He obviously was trying to alert the golfer to the *entire* situation: the wind, the turf, the slope, the hazards, the distractions, the complete scene in which he was going to act.

This preliminary advice is well suited to the process of home buying. You will be operating in a total environment of time as well as space. So, look around you. Then look backward and forward in time. The backward look will give you the history and reputation of the neighborhood where you are looking; the forward look will help you dramatize and actualize your own placement and participation in the neighborhood. Look all around you.

You must start with some knowledge of the neighborhood characteristics. Typically, most cities have their apartment-house areas (now perhaps changing partially into condominiums), their town houses, their small bungalows that were the subdivisions of the twenties and thirties, their post-World War II tracts on the outskirts, their "gold coasts" or premium residential areas, and, of course, their transitional or mixed areas and their slums.

The technical problems of shopping for older properties is gone into later in separate chapters on mechanical evaluation. Your overriding concern at the outset, though, is to seek out those areas where land appreciation will be the greatest. Choice residential locations are always scarce. With inflation destined to continue indefinitely to a greater or lesser degree, this limited premium property should continue to rise in value. Caution is necessary, though, for factors such as social deterioration, an increase in crime and overall citywide decline can cause a dramatic plummeting of values.

Land Costs

Whether you are looking at a property in the city, a subdivision or in the country, develop a procedure for evaluating it.

1. Know where it is—tract number, identification, direction from town, roads serving it, services, etc.
2. Know which way it faces—direction, prevailing wind.
3. Know its size, zoning, place in master plan.
4. Know what is around it, zoning, place in master plan.
5. Know the nature of the street in front of it.
6. Know the taxes, assessments.
7. Know its future as to all of these points.

Real estate salesmen talk constantly about the properties they are showing, but few buyers ask penetrating questions and proceed to take notes in earnest, most preferring to bask in the temporary, quasi-social ambience, enjoying being talked to so solicitously and entertained for an hour or so.

Making such a substantial investment is major-league business, and so, particularly, is this matter of land cost. It, more than anything else, may determine future appreciation, so make serious business out of the questions and note taking.

Anticipate Decline

A city government—specifically, the planning department, the planning commission, and its superior, the city council—can do much to either bring about decline of an area or to prevent its decline. If there is not sufficient industrial, commercial or agricultural vitality to a community, and if that community is not a satellite of a city where there is, there is little they can do to prevent eventual overall decline of values except by attracting those elements. Once given a viable balance of local economic activity, certain areas of the community are protected by zoning regulations and other restrictions, such as lot size, building setbacks, height limitations and, sometimes, architectural controls.

The pressure against too restrictive controls is often exerted by developers lobbying for small lots, cluster or common-wall housing, zero front-yard setbacks, minimum street widths, off-street parking (but not necessarily two-car garage parking), and unusable small green areas. They do this because of spiraling land costs and the need to have less land hold more people.

A wizardlike planning commission would arrange a variegated residential complex with all categories represented, but none suffering from disastrous juxtaposition with one of the more dense uses. Alas! All types of zoning must at some place touch different types. Also, wizards are scarce these days, especially on planning boards.

Make it your business to know the zoning conditions that do and *will* affect the location of interest to you. Become an expert in this aspect of the local political scene. Talk with the people behind the planning department desks, ask to see a current zoning map, talk with a planning commissioner. Be assured that the master plan of the future buttresses the land investment you are about to make. Look far ahead. Project into the future.

Then use your eyes. Look around you. A neighboring area may have gone to seed. Is it capable of being rejuvenated? Sometimes if you can discover facts that indicate a general refurbishing is coming due to zone change, new ownership, new capital, new development, higher taxes favoring a beneficial liquidation by a former owner, you will be gaining strong profit beachheads in the battle for land appreciation.

Georgetown in Washington, D.C., is an example of a revitalized community, and there are many more across the nation.

Some "Don'ts" on City Looking

Think cautiously and *twice* about view sites, including hillsides and homes not part of an identifiable and desirable neighborhood. These properties are often difficult to finance and refinance. Also, they can be difficult to resell.

Avoid canyon homes if you are interested in maximizing appreciation. They are often vulnerable to flooding, fire, high fire-insurance rates and poor resale. Streets are often narrow and plagued with fast traffic. Drainage problems usually affect building sites, streets and sidewalks. Utilities and other services are often minimal.

Do not expect much appreciation from land located near the base of a dam, under the takeoff or approach pattern of an airport, over an earthquake fault system or near a freeway. The same is true of property that is just at the edge of a transition from one use (say, R-3, or apartment-house use) to another (such as commercial or industrial). Investors, lenders and future buyers of your position generally want protection or a "buffer" between themselves and a differing use.

Do not buy a high-priced house in a medium-priced area; conversely, seek out properties for sale that are surrounded by *better* houses than you are being offered.

Neighborhoods

Neighborhoods have reputations just like people. In older existing neighborhoods, it is helpful to steep yourself in their good and bad points, because that will more or less be the same characterization that obtains when you ultimately attempt to sell your property. If you are shopping in a new subdivision, there may have been comparably priced and sized homes sold previously nearby that can provide you with some indicators. Otherwise, you will simply have to pay careful attention to the unfolding sales situation, listen carefully to what you are told and attempt to exercise the best judgment you can.

This same attentiveness holds for streets. It is amazing how streets that can appear so similar to the uninitiated can be called so positvely "good" or "bad" by experts, with fairly logical reasons given to support those descriptions that would never occur to an outsider. Such things as extra-large lots by even a few feet, alleys in the rear, no through traffic, no appreciable street grade (thus minimizing use of low gears in vehicles), no bus stop directly in front (reducing low gears and exhaust), not too many young children all of the same age, not too many old people, not too many dogs, etc.—all are important in ranking the quality of streets.

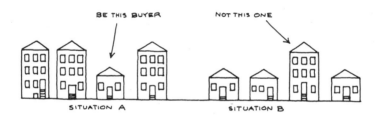

Distance from Work

Much is said about the desirability of locating a home near schools, library, post office, shops, church, playground, etc., so that children can avail themselves easily of these facilities and so the woman of the house does not have to be a full-time chauffeur.

Once, when a farmer's hogs were observed laboriously gnawing at dried corncobs, he was asked why he did not grind up the cobs into silage so as to make less arduous the hogs' job of wresting some nutrition out of the tough cobs. "The hogs' time isn't worth anything," answered the farmer; "but *my* time and equipment *is.*"

Although this is perhaps at first glance too cynical a thought to apply to the husband, wife, or the children of a household, it does point out a seeming imbalance in our philosophy of home orientation. It seems too bad that the breadwinner of a household works over half of his waking hours, and then frequently must spend an additional hour or two commuting to and from his house to his place of work. When some of this time can be recaptured by reading or doing work while riding on public transportation, commuting time is not entirely lost. Where he is enslaved to the wheel of an automobile, his eyes riveted to the bumper ahead of him, his plight is more pitiable.

Try to reduce time spent in automobile commuting. Just add up the time spent in one day, multiply by 260 working days and stand by for a jolt. Four hundred hours a year would be quite normal, and that is a shocking amount of time. It is in excess of two weeks—lost, completely lost.

Bernard Berenson said at a late age that he wished he could stand with his cap in his hand begging passersby for their wasted minutes. His work in art research could have benefited the world. What would he have thought about the monumental waste of man's time behind the wheel of an automobile?

This waste poses a strong argument for location of a home within the central part of a city, by the way, and should not be overlooked.

A Fount of Information

One excellent source as to what portions of a city are the most desirable is a loan officer at a savings and loan association serving the immediate area. This executive can wear a gimlet eye when approached by a borrower needing mortgage money for a hillside or canyon property. The risk of foundation slippage or settling, storm damage, mud, fire, and sluggishness of resale and high

incidents of repossession may have given him and his loan committee a very clear idea of the vulnerability inherent in such
properties.

Security

Much has been thought and written about security in recent
years, particularly within the cities where crime has proliferated.
No single neighborhood seems exempt from this plague. Walled,
guarded, TV- and helicopter-scrutinized communities offer a type
of solution, but these isolated compounds are expensive to maintain and beg the reflection that the residents themselves are near
to being prisoners within their own high walls. In the long run, this
cannot bode well.

The same kind of reputation that applies in ranking neighborhoods economically, socially and by other criteria of enjoyment
and appreciation also applies with respect to crime. You should
ask questions of police and municipal authorities about crime as it
relates to that specific area. Thorough records are kept on bur-
glaries and muggings, and in the minds of the police there are areas
where this is more of a hazard than others.

Here again, it is question of not leading with your chin. Sometimes it is best to eschew the attractive old brownstone in the
"borderline" area just because you will not be able to venture out
of your front door at night. It is hard to think of another negative
factor that would damage the salability (not to mention your
interim use and enjoyment of the house) more at such time as you
might wish to sell it.

The City as an Environment for Children

Jane Jacobs is a writer known for championing the small,
eclectic, often overlooked vestiges of old-fashioned village life as it
persists in certain venerable but healthy residential areas of old

cities. She refers in *The Death and Life of Great American Cities* to the growing child's view of a community that includes the figures of women *and* men—adults!—in constant daily pursuit of their own activities, not as servants to the children.

Storekeepers, minor businessmen and women, professional people, farmers, tradesmen, all are moving about in constant view as symbols of the perhaps absent father, who may be working at a greater distance in the city. These pockets of business and service and arts give versatility and continuity to a community that otherwise is just a collection of bedrooms and home TV parlors. Mrs. Jacobs points out that new cities and communities would benefit in lower crime rates and, overall, more wholesome environments for children by integrating commercial establishments (particularly one-man, small commercial businesses) with residential zoning. Small cities and rural areas often retain this quality of a small-town hub or nexus of combined adult and juvenile intercourse.

Bring yourself to prize highly these neighborhood shops and service facilities not merely as step-saving conveniences, but as the very valuable and precious assets they are. They help keep a balance between the adult sexes, and they create an invaluable village within a city in the finest sense of that phrase.

Future Changes—For the Better

New stores, new businesses, new factories, new industrial, commercial and agricultural activity of any kind is important for you to know about. It will all affect the value of nearby land. Attune your antennae to every wisp and scrap of positive information. Become an expert. Talk to the building department, chamber of commerce, savings and loan association officers, bank. Ask them all about what is going on in the area that you are interested in that can possibly affect the value there. Take notes on what you find out.

Checklist of Available Sources of Community Information
____City offices:
____Building department
____Planning department
____Engineering or public works department
____Chamber of commerce
____Savings and loans
____Bank

Often a particular area of the country can be particularly resistant to a period of severe national economic downturn—again a protection for your investment in a specific property. This is possible not only because the community possesses qualities of integral economic vitality and multiplicity that save it from a generally moribund situation, but also because it harbors its own vital activity of growth that is powerful enough to stave off the pervasive national economic distress. Look for such a quality.

Microcosmically, this self-generated potential exists even in neighborhoods within a city, in subdivisions within other sub-divisions, and in acreage in the country situated among other country properties. This self-direction exists because the positive qualities are there and keep hoisting land values higher and higher.

Points to Remember in City Shopping
1. Buy what *sells well* and the appreciation will take care of itself.
2. Emphasize *location* within the city.
3. Give lower priority to the size and function of the house itself and higher priority to the land and its location in order to maximize appreciation.
4. Heed the experience of *lenders:* they are in the business, basically, of evaluating equities.
5. Check on the crime rate in the area you are interested in.

6
LOOKING NEAR
THE CITY—
SUBDIVISIONS,
COUNTRY PROPERTY

Subdivisions

The main thrust of new-housing promotion that the prospective home buyer is aware of emanates from the various subdivisions rimming the city or town. As opposed to single-house selling, this mass marketing of houses is a well-organized, well-advertised, and in some cases, well-produced effort, beautifully calculated to magnetize the prospect with (1) a great deal of elaboration as to location advantage, (2) a playing up of any nearby recreational facilities, and (3) an enumeration of house features with sole emphasis (naturally!) on the plus features.

As to the description of the locale, this will doubtless concentrate on convenience, abundance of service facilities, plus school and cultural possibilities. A careful look at the reality of the location will probably reveal a heavy weighting toward social and recreational pursuits. While these are assuredly of immediate interest to most members of the family, they do not necessarily aid the objective of land appreciation. Rather, the general location of the subdivision in total and its relative position in relation to other subdivisions of comparable price structure is a more controlling factor in land appreciation.

For example, Subdivision 1 is located quite close to the core of the city with easy access to transportation, shops, schools and theaters, but yet nested in a gently rolling countryside (not hillside!), with large-sized, irregularly shaped lots, eccentric street patterns, underground utilities, and plenty of large trees with tough prohibitions on tearing them down. Compare it critically with Subdivision 2, which has comparably priced houses, equally large lots, a pitch-and-putt golf course, community swimming pool, sauna and tennis courts (for fifty or sixty houses), but it is located farther from town on relatively flat land, with no mature trees, and a nondeveloped tract adjacent to it whose zoning and residential density have not yet been determined. Subdivision 1 should be the better long-term investment.

Remember to project your analysis of how a subdivision will perform in the real estate market *as far as possible into the future.* Remember that to be successful when there are many more subdivisions around it, it needs people who will pay a premium— that is, more than you are paying—for a location within that subdivision sometime in the future. Try to keep this dynamic or "unfolding" aspect of land development in mind. Most sub-

SUBDIVISION I   SUBDIVISION 2

divisions sell fairly well the first time around. Then new competition is attracted, and sometimes in staggering quantity. Ask yourself, how will that subdivision sell? Look far ahead. Project into the future.

What Facilities Are Nearby?

Unlike the established, older part of the city, the facilities upon which you will depend will most likely not be as convenient, and in some cases may not be available, to certain tract subdivisions. Here is a checklist of facilities that would be desirable to have within convenient walking or bicycling distance:

Wife or husband's work	Bookstore
School	Laundry and cleaner
Police and fire departments	Playground
Train, bus, or rapid transit	Bank
Library	Barber shop, beauty parlor
Hospital and medical building	Restaurants
Service station with mechanic	Church
Drugstore with pharmacist	Market
Motion-picture theater	Community club or gathering place
	Specialty shops

The ability of a large subdivider to sell houses successfully from which an automobile *must* be used to take advantage of three-quarters of the community's "facilities" listed above remains a mystery. Such dependence on the car automatically makes a chauffeur out of the wife and often the husband as well. It also, in the philosophy of Jane Jacobs, creates an unreal world in which children view almost everybody around them as either women or their own kind. Male adults are a nighttime phenomenon.

Schools

The application of property tax dollars within those communities where the dollars are collected may shortly undergo a constitutional test. But the quality of education, including existing buildings, teaching staff, facilities and reputation, plus statewide and local ranking as to other schools, etc., goes a long way in determining land value. A community boasting good schools is going to have quite an edge over one with a struggling program of education.

This type of analysis should be more or less self-evident, but it will pay to inquire directly of knowledgeable parents, clergymen, chamber of commerce people and the like. Really know what you are talking about by thoroughly investigating the school system and rating it high on your list of assets supportive of land value. Ask for the list of schools within the state that shows the latest ranking of students passing the college board entrance examinations. The ranking of the nearby schools compared with others in the city and county will give some strong clue to the quality of education.

On this subject, a very fruitful source of information on the juvenile picture would be to talk with the police department or county probation officers about the comparative qualities of the various communities. Crime statistics should be at their fingertips, and what they can tell you about the higher and lower figures in various parts of the community might be quite enlightening.

Busing of School Children

Since it is outside the realm of concern of this book, we will not undertake an analysis of the pros and cons of busing schoolchildren. It is obvious that the busing of schoolchildren to remote schools is a hotly controversial issue, and it can have a substantial effect on the resale value of your property. Whatever your sentiments on the issue itself, it is impossible to believe that property values are aided where this situation exists. So from the monastic isolation of your own personal quest for maximum potential in real estate enhancement, consider the realities of busing as it can apply to you and your children. The distances involved, if too great, can be a drawback. On the other hand, local "pooled" facilities may produce an upgrading of instruction.

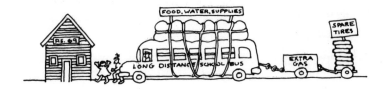

Services

Find out about police and fire protection. In some areas, fire insurance is expensive because of remoteness from a fire station and/or remoteness from a fire hydrant. Learn about the protection you can expect and make note of it in comparing other communities.

Health services are important, too. You will want to know where the nearest emergency hospital is, not only for childhood emergencies, but for adult ones as well. Is there an intensive care unit at the hospital for care of a sudden heart-attack victim? How good is ambulance service in the area?

The nearness of a good service-station operator is worth its weight in gold. This is not to praise an operator who can merely pump gas and wash cars, but to single out that talented, begrimed worthy who can really fix automobiles, tires, install mufflers, grind valves and adjust carburetors. Such a haven can save hours of time and inconvenience in ferrying cars to and from a downtown dealer's service department, where appointments have to be made and lines gotten into, where the only palliative is a TV waiting room with dog-eared, cheap magazines.

Utilities—Gas, Electric, Telephone, TV

These vital services are placed underground in most new communities. The lack of telephone poles with black wires festooned to the residences below greatly improves the appearance of a community. Trees, then, can vie with roof lines in forming a pleasing skyline. Of course, in older sections of a city the poles usually cannot be avoided. You just have to live with them.

Ask about sewers. Being connected to one gives you a much more secure feeling than having to rely on a cesspool or septic tank. The maintenance problem is all but eliminated by being connected to a city sewer system, and with a little vigilance as to root growth and other possible blockages in your own house "soil" system, you should have no further concern in that area of service.

Water damage and runoff are important as well. Walk around, and, if possible, visit the property when it is raining or right after a rain to see that the location is able to dispel the water that falls on it.

Through Traffic

A cul-de-sac is ideal, because it presents a quiet street situation with no through traffic, and except for the occasional stranger who has to turn around, it is traveled only by the residents of the street and those providing them services.

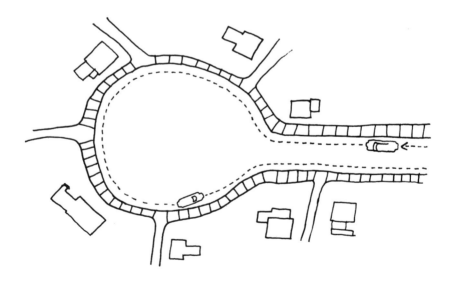

Next best is a street with very little traffic on it. Ask about traffic that might be a hazard to children, make backing out of a driveway difficult and dangerous, and present noise problems and make crime more likely just by virtue of carrying more automobiles.

Television, both uhf and vhf, is vital to resale even if you and your family are not addicted to it. There are few areas in the country now that can neither receive television signals in the normal way or by cable connection, but be sure you check this out and satisfy yourself that good reception is available.

Taxes

High property taxes are damaging to land appreciation out of proportion to the actual differences in such taxes. They can hurt noticeably if nearby property is available to future buyers at lower tax rates because of differing appraisal techniques, differing incorporation, etc.

Psychologically, property taxes should not be as odious as certain other taxes. They are earmarked for predominantly local uses, most of which directly benefit the property owner and his family. Although there are city and county bureaucracies, to be sure, their costs have, in general, a lower percentage relationship to funds disbursed than the state or national government. A recent tax bill includes the following items:

County library	County mosquito abatement
County cemetery	County water district
County transit district	County lighting maintenance
County flood control	Education
County harbor district	County—general
City—general	

Now, insofar as local and county governments and their various administrative boards are thrifty and effective, it is pretty hard to quarrel with the general *use* to which these taxes are put. This is a consideration apart from the moot argument concerning the percentage loading of such taxes as applied to the owners of property, or the fact that unfair distribution of proceeds might occur, as is argued in the case of education.

The smallest and most purely communal group would have to suppose some education and would have to deal with a mosquito or two. This type of local responsibility is not fairly ranked alongside support of large, bureaucratic, governmental entities at state and national levels.

Nevertheless, the amount of property tax paid can be a significant deterrent in reselling a property. Make yourself take the time to research the surrounding tax structure in order to assure yourself that you are not getting in a position that is relatively *costlier* than nearby areas, since heavy taxation can render a location unpopular when it comes to resale. Unfortunately, that kind of reputation can attach itself to a community even though the differential is relatively minor. So it goes. That is the way with gossip.

1984—The Increased Use of the Home

For better or for worse, television has brought entertainment, albeit a rather passive and mass-catered form, back into the home. Additionally, many business firms have experimented with a four-day workweek, and some union contracts already provide for three days off a week. It can be argued that this extra leisure time merely means an expansion of second homes and recreational pursuits. However, for most people it must surely spell out an increased use of the home. In studying floor plans, therefore, this newly expanding use will be an important consideration. It is also important with respect to the location of the home.

To have a home that is to be a truly enjoyable place to spend a great deal of time, it should be located where it is relatively free from noise. This refers to all kinds of mechanized noise—airplanes, trains, automobile traffic, buses—and also to the noise of people and animals. This is difficult to achieve in a neighborhood, of course. However, there is no point in asking for trouble. At least evaluate the sound problem and make a decision with your eyes wide open.

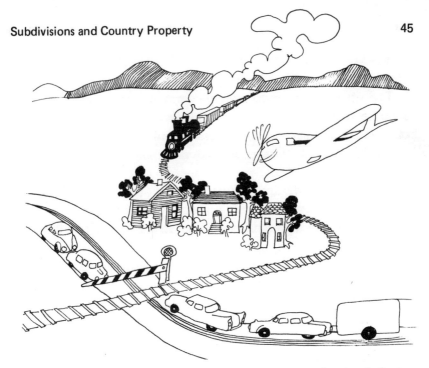

Minimization of noise, however, is just one of several factors that will heighten enjoyment of this increased leisure time. Room to expand, pleasant neighbors, the convenient facilities already mentioned, a place to get out of doors in privacy, an area outside in which to maintain cars and boats or to work on other hobbies, plenty of separation from others within the home, security, a good area for growing flowers and vegetables, good community activity if you crave this, and possibly a local club of some sort.

The pub or "local" that abounds in the British Isles, and the small cafes, coffee bars and bars that are everywhere in Europe, perform a function that is not properly filled by either the typical U. S. country club, the cocktail bar or the local restaurants. It is a rare community that has a truly amiable common gathering place, but if you are fortunate enough to find one, rank such a facility high on the plus side. In the past, the town square helped serve this function, and in certain communities that have not grown too big or too fast, these have been preserved. They now help in some small measure to provide a focal point for community identi-fication.

Community Restrictions

There are sometimes restrictions in neighborhoods and communities that transcend building department regulations and zoning provisions by the planning department. Be sure to familiarize yourself with any such restrictions. Usually they are imposed on an area by the original developer, not to stifle the imagination or creative desire of the residents, but to insure a certain amount of discipline, since we cannot all be relied upon to possess a properly developed and compatible aesthetic sense.

One of the nation's most highly disciplined sets of design criteria has been developed by the Irvine Company for its gilt-edged community of Linda Isle in Newport Beach, California. It has been in effect for some years now. Despite the fact that the lots average 50 by 100 feet in size and that sideyards are 4 feet, leaving only 8 feet between houses, the planning has paid off. The visual effect is orderly and pleasing. So it is difficult to find fault with such a rigorous attention to materials and their treatment. A list of some of the architectural restrictions can be found in Appendix A.

The Country

At one time it may be that a farmer has a lot or two for sale, another time it might be that an old estate on the edge of town is being broken up as a five- or ten-lot subdivision. Then again, a small farm might be for sale with a farmhouse and some outbuildings. Here, from time to time, lies an opportunity in land investment plus good living besides. Keep your eyes open to the possibilities of buying a house or some land in the country. It is a pleasant way of life and offers some distinct advantages besides the possibility of land appreciation. It is an excellent place to raise children. The country, with the chance to have animals and raise fresh fruit and vegetables, can provide a heaven-sent seedbed for resourcefulness and creativity, a responsible, independent way of thinking and living that is preferred by many over the seemingly stereotyped pattern of suburban living.

There are some real problems attached to country living, though. Social contacts are sparse and more difficult to develop, unless one makes an effort to extend oneself in the community's affairs. Normal lending· may be restricted, with loan ratios approaching only 50 percent of the value of the farm. This is because the savings and loan associations commit most of their available real estate loans to residential lending, where the improvements represent a high percentage of the value of the total package. As the value percentage of improvements shifts toward the value of the land, the lendable percentage shrinks. Therefore, 70 to 80 percent loans on farm homes and country properties are rare.

More imagination is required in seeking out a lot or farm in the country, because comparable standards are less available. Certainly there is no mass merchandising of country properties, or we would be calling it a subdivision. Instead, one faces a parcel-by-parcel evaluation and a lot of fact digging in order to ascertain real worth and probable appreciation potential.

And finally, be disabused of any notion about creating income from small farms. Farming is a full-time job requiring up-to-date equipment, ample working capital, much technical knowledge and enough land to create low-unit costs for efficient crop and live-stock production—an almost impossible undertaking for an amateur. Moreover, many good men with all of these things going for them still lose money at it. They may make up for this—and more!—over the years with the appreciation of their land. So, no need to weep for them.

Continue to place your emphasis on land appreciation, with any light farming ranking along with sports and hobbies as a pleasant family-group activity.

7
WHY USE A BROKER?

Surely, you say, by reading the ads and following up on them yourself you can save the broker's 5 or 6 percent commission. Wrong! At least it is wrong from the standpoint of fully covering the market, of fully exploring the possible houses for sale.

By not using a broker you are limiting your exposure to only those owners who do their own advertising, which is quite restrictive indeed. Moreover, a broker is helpful in developing your sense of comparable values. He has many listings, makes many contacts and several sales. All of this knowledge can relate to your understanding of your own house-hunting problem. It can help you make a better offer when you find what you want. The investment potential can be maximized. Someone once said in jest that "An expert is a person who avoids the small errors as he sweeps on to the grand fallacy," and it is true that you should not rely on any broker, expert as he might be, to make the final decision. That must be your responsibility, arrived at with the broker's aid.

Here, in this chapter, we develop the many ways in which a broker can assist you, if only you know how to use him correctly.

What Broker to Use?

Try to find someone who is physically located near the areas in which you are interested. If you can get a recommendation of a good broker, then pursue it. Otherwise, use your own judgment in studying the amount and *quality* of advertising placed by the competing brokers and take a chance by contacting one whose thematic approach makes sense. There will be no great problem in changing offices later on if you fail to communicate. In fact, be aggressive about switching brokers if things are not going to your satisfaction, since it is much easier to do this than to waste hour after hour with an unimaginative salesperson.

In most states, the term *broker* refers to one who has the full selling license. A real estate salesman has only the beginning license and has presumably not had the training to be qualified to the extent that a broker has. Each licensed office must have one or more full brokers with their licenses posted. Salesmen can only work under a broker and are responsible to him in all of their activities.

Whom Does He Represent?

The broker stands in a peculiar ethical position. He is supposed to represent both sides—buyer and seller alike. However, it does not always work out that way. To see what happens, you must picture the broker's file bulging with static, paper listings. In front of him sits you—the *buyer!*—and at that particular moment in time you symbolize the only being on earth that harbors the genesis of a sale. All of his hopes are momentarily focused on you. You are a living, breathing buyer, and he will usually bend over backwards to work in your behalf to find you the house you want.

Learn to use this built-in magnetism to your advantage. Do not yoke yourself to a spiritless plowhorse and be pulled around to various meaningless offerings as your salesman waits for your spark to ignite. Instead, begin by preparing yourself, then by preparing him to absorb your exact requirements.

An old story describes a farmer's response when asked why he constantly smote his mule with a 2 by 4 prior to issuing an order. "Why, to gain his attention," he said. Very few people are good listeners, and this is particularly true of salespeople. They are very intent upon the next thing they are going to say. Prime yourself in this area of insensitivity. Extend your antennae so as to recognize a bad listener, and switch salespeople immediately or fly to a new office if it is uncomfortable to change within the same office. Be merciless about this and you will benefit. For nobody but a good listener will be able to fully absorb your requirements and not show you things you will immediately have to reject.

Different Types of Listings

Exclusive Listings.

These are listings where the seller agrees to sell only through a particular broker's office. Usually the broker has had to assure the seller that he would push the property very hard, spend money on advertising, and really mount an impressive sales effort. If the broker's office sells these exclusive properties they retain all of the commission. But he generally "subs out" these exclusive listings to other brokers on a 50-50 split of the commission.

Open Listings.

These are given by the seller to as many offices as possible; whichever office sells the property gets the full commission. Open listings are much used for properties that do not require special, intensified selling or advertising, like a vacant lot or a house on a desirable street or in a desirable neighborhood. As the buyer, you are much less likely to know what other buying activity or offers have been made on an open-listed property, because not all information is funneling through one broker's office.

Multiple Listings.

This is a service of publishing and sharing listings that is active in most larger communities. It is usually controlled by a local board of realtors. An essential question to ask your broker at your very first meeting is: "Is there a really vital multiple listing system in this community?"

One reason the multiple system does not always work is that too great a disparity may exist in the size and potency of brokers' offices. That is, the larger, more effective ones may command most of the listings and, therefore, most of the sales. They will balk at sharing their listings with numerous shoebox operators. In such a market, you will not be able to utilize the multiple listings with great effectiveness, and you will need to determine if the one broker you start with is of a stature where he is getting all the good "shared" listings from the other major offices. If not, you will simply have to grit your teeth and cover the other larger offices separately.

If the multiple-listing service is a good one, those files in your broker's office are an excellent starting place to test some of your requirements and, incidentally, to better implant them in your broker's head.

Write Down Your Requirements

Write down what you consider important to you in a home, even if you do not plan to show the list to the broker. What this will help you do is to acquire practice and ease in stating your requirements clearly so they are lucidly transmittable to the broker. If you simply will not buy a house without morning sun in the kitchen or breakfast room, or with a detached garage, or without a swimming pool (or the place to put one), or within a certain distance from stores, write down those things. Then number them in order of their priority.

The First Meeting, or, Spending Time to Conserve Time

You should plan for your initial meeting *at the broker's office.* Allow plenty of time to go over your requirements. Then turn to the files of listings and photographs in his office. Even request prior to the meeting that he screen the listings beforehand to further conserve your time. Above all, do not permit the broker to hustle you off, his coat pocket bulging with keys to houses that are not previously qualified in conversation.

Sit quietly in his office going over your notes, gaining more and more of the broker's understanding of your requirements, examining the written listings and photographs and discarding the unsuitable as a waste of time.

There must be a special hell somewhere for writers of sales manuals who preach that if you can just get the client to *see* something, he will want it. It is like saying that you, the buyer, could not tell a bad egg without laying one. Furthermore, it is irresponsible management of your own time to permit yourself to be trundled around to houses that are not discussed beforehand. Sitting in the broker's car listening to him present houses that he is going to show you without screening them previously is wasteful. Simply refuse to do it! *Force* the real estate man to do his homework and to prove to you that he has done it by going over his offerings in advance. This gives you the opportunity to reiterate your requirements. You can say, "Don't you remember, I have to have a maid's room."

What about Price Range?

The single, most important element of house hunting is the price objective. As a buyer, you are pretty certain what you can afford to pay for a house, yet there are several variables for you to consider.

1. Softness in asking price, due to:
   a. Length of time on the market
   b. Current problems or attitude of seller
   c. General market conditions as they now affect seller
2. Flexibility in lending, by:
   a. Increase in replace first trust deed or mortgage
   b. Possibility of second trust deed carried by seller
3. Reselling portion of property or dividing
4. Greater appreciation factors that offset higher initial price paid

Do not brainwash the broker too severely on the matter of price limitation. Do not wear blinders throughout the vital processing of listed homes. *Do not be afraid to look above your price range!*

If you want a $50,000 house but can buy a much better one for $65,000 that has an extra lot that is marketable at $15,000, see if the owner will carry a second trust deed for long enough to let you resell the lot. You are obviously better off if the house in the second case is superior. Often the listings are filed according to price, and you can therefore see why the broker might not show you the $65,000 offering if you limited him too severely on price.

How to Find Out If Property Is for Sale

If you think a house might be for sale but have no way of finding out, the broker can find this out for you through the title company. Some larger offices even maintain their own files of the tax assessment records and can follow up in these possibilities right on the spot. This is particularly valuable and timesaving where you are inquiring about several properties.

Emphasize Resale

Dwell with the broker at length on the subject of appreciation and resale, sometimes called the "aftermarket." Stifle his tendency to think in cozy "ma and pa" terms about your future shelter. Make him rise to the occasion of offering investment advice. Despite his shortcomings as a general investment counselor, for better or worse, you are relying on him to steer you into a lifetime of debt. Inspire him to do the very finest job he can for the preservation of your equity. Maybe his talents will expand to fulfill the demand.

Do not expect him to say he can resell the house immediately for you and make you a profit. That would be comforting, if true. Rather, get him to express this appreciation and resale potential in terms of broad market progress, comparative offerings, and the future. After all, he is usually in the business of appraising real estate as well. His own office partners gossip constantly about the relative merits of their listings. Get him to open up in the range of your interests. One or two of his offerings are sure to bubble to the top as being better buys than the rest.

8
INTENSIFYING
THE SEARCH

How to Look at a House

Assume that the homework and office work have been done, and the offerings have been sifted down to a choice few. This preparatory work might well be done by one person working with the broker at his office. If the broker is a sharp one when it comes to actually inspecting the properties, he will try to conserve his own time by asking the couple to look together. He will not want to do a lot of house showing that he knows has to be repeated, although he is often frustrated in this by the husband's working hours. As a result, he usually has to be satisfied with a preliminary screening of initial offerings by the wife. The couple then follows up on the survivors of her first visits.

With the preparation work behind you, there are some ideal inspection conditions. It is very helpful, for example, if the broker can schedule a time when the *owner is not present*. While some sellers have the sensitivity to take a half-hour walk during an inspection of their house, others hover and loiter around the house, pointing out the closets, perhaps cooking cabbage on the stove, or, worst of all, sitting in a darkened room watching daytime television.

If looking gets serious on a particular house, another valuable procedure is for each person of a couple to look at the house alone. Yes, alone. When a couple is together they either react with mutuality or lack of mutuality, and either reaction is distracting to a thorough study of the house. In mutuality, they are in the role of "couple," acting in concert, listening as a couple, relating to the inspection process as a sort of Siamese twin, expressing "couple-ness"—something apart from the two critical and judgment-making people they are. Conversely, in a condition of lack of mutuality or disharmony, they are involved in their own common frustration and contentiousness, further aggravated by strange, demanding surroundings and people—plus the pressure of imminent decision making.

Ideally, when the choice narrows to one or two properties and the offering stage approaches, the man and woman would each go alone and be left alone in the house. That, after all, will most closely simulate their future relationship to it. There are plenty of times for the husband and wife to discuss the house together, but what is emphasized here is the value of inspecting and absorbing the premises so that the mental picture and the "spatial feel" of the place are solidly in one's own mind, so that you as an individual *experience the house.*

Check the House at Night

A noted writer who had had bad luck with noisy apartments took the matter so seriously that in relocating again he arranged to work for a portion of three different days in a prospective apartment. Upon finding it quiet enough, he executed a lease and moved in. The first night revealed that a family of eight who were all absent during the day at various offices, schools, nurseries, etc., returned to the roost and raised all hell until they fell into a

belated slumber. So, too, with a house: Why be blind to the fact
that a noisy pet is kept next door that only opens up at night
when his owner goes out to dinner or leaves for night school or a
job? Or that a neighbor keeps a lighted machine shop active in the
garage from seven until eleven at night? Or cranks up a ham radio
outfit that upsets television sets for blocks around? Guard against
these surprises by getting to know your prospective house at night.

The Broker's Other Services

Financing

Never is a broker so anxious to serve you as he is just prior to a
possible sale. It is his finest hour. Take advantage of this. One of
the areas where he can be of greatest service is in generating a good
range of financing possibilities.

Taxes, assessments, bonds and present financing information—
this data is conveniently spelled out on his written listing form.
However, information on refinancing (increasing the existing
loan), transfer charges, possibility of a new loan with another
lender, payoff charges on the old loan, owner financing by means
of a new first or second note and trust deed carried by the seller,
all need to be developed.

In this connection, an inspection and appraisal will have to be
made by any potential lender, even the existing lender, if he is
being asked to increase the financing to the maximum allowable
(about 80 percent of the selling price). All this requires coordin-
ation, appointments, availability of keys, running around and
following up on information required by the loan officer. This is
all part of a good broker's capabilities. If you are serious about a
house, and if your own time means anything to you, get the
broker to help you with financing early in the game.

Painting, Repairs, Remodeling.

If the house has to be repainted, a room added, or other
structural or remodeling work undertaken, get the broker to

obtain an estimate for the work. You may wish to get another estimate later on yourself, or you may not even have the work done, but use his time and energy and his ambition for a deal to meet the painter and builder on the job and take care of this initial estimating for you.

If you want architectural plans for study, there may be some around. Ask the broker to locate these, if possible, and get you a copy. You can then study them in terms of your own needs, doing an overlay with the furnishings you already have and seeing if the floor plan is really going to work for you.

City and County Restrictions.

Put the broker to work *confirming* the correctness of the zoning represented, unearthing the exact wording of any restrictions or any activity by the city or county that might affect the property, such as the widening of a street or the loss of lot area by conscription, condemnation, easement, freeway construction or the like.

Do Your Own Research in Advertising

Owner Advertising.

Occasionally an individual will attempt his own advertising. However, a profile of him might reveal an independent, tough-minded cuss who is relatively inflexible when it comes to negotiating price and terms. On the other hand, there could be the strong possibility that the property is a dog that no broker would touch at the price advertised. The very fact that the owner is trying to avoid the 5 or 6 percent commission is a clue to his rigidity of mind and his dedication to wringing every penny out of the property.

Vacant property is an exception to this negative statement about owner advertising. It can often be presented effectively in advertising as well as by posted signs. It is available for easy inspection, need not be shown by appointment, and offers few problems in effecting a sales contract once the price is negotiated.

Advertising by Brokers.

Advertising for houses is mostly placed by real estate offices, both in classified and display ads. It can be very instructional in the house-hunting process. Not only can you get a feel of prices as they relate to a specific area or neighborhood, but the quantity of ads is helpful in assaying the ebb and flow of the so-called buyers' and sellers' markets.

Advertising is often a clue to the relative aggressiveness of certain brokerage offices. Also, in addition to the multiple listings, a large amount of advertising out of a single office can indicate a large group of exclusive listings. A broker will frequently obtain an exclusive listing that he is eventually going to place into the multiple-listing service, but he will have an understanding with the seller that he may have a grace period of, say, thirty to sixty days, during which he agrees to advertise the property heavily, hold open houses on it, and attempt to sell it out of his own office.

This is why it is often necessary to cover more than one brokerage office in a thorough search, and why it is helpful to keep abreast with all significant advertising during that period.

Trying to Classify Buyers' and Sellers' Markets

Real estate markets (that is, the character of day-to-day buying and selling) can, during a particular period, appear to be what is often referred to as either a buyers' or sellers' market. Presumably, the house hunter is in luck if it is a buyers' market, inasmuch as that indicates an oversupply of houses and suggests that he will get better deals. The scarcity of houses or an overabundance of buyers makes a sellers' market, where those grudgingly disposing of the few houses that come into the market need only name their price in order to get it.

Needless to say, the situation is usually much more complicated than that, when you consider that you could have very few listings of houses but, concurrently, very few buyers; or, conversely, you might have many listings but legions of buyers. What would these markets be called? Actually, you and your desire and your own aggressiveness for a house will make it what kind of a market it is. Prepare in advance, do your homework, motivate the broker to do his homework, plan, look ahead, and you will find what you want. Later we will discuss how you can adapt your offer to the illusory qualities of the buyers' or sellers' market.

What about Buying Directly from the Owner?

If you come across a house through advertising, or a lot that you want to buy without a broker, you will lack the forms and documents to get the deal down on paper. You can work with a reliable escrow company, the escrow office of your bank or the escrow office of the savings and loan that has the loan on the property to solve this problem. They will prepare any documents you need in order to close the deal. More about that will come up in the chapter about escrows. Briefly, you will need to have prepared:

1. Escrow instructions
2. Grant deed
3. Note and trust deed to seller, if any
4. Statement of identity for the title company
5. Loan documents from institutional lender, including:
   a. Loan application
   b. Financial statement (personal)
   c. Miscellaneous papers

It is always wise to consult a lawyer in any involved agreement, but most sophisticated attorneys do not expect to be drawn into their clients' routine property transactions in states where title companies operate.

9
WHAT STYLE OF HOUSE DO YOU WANT?

Style—What Is It?

Very little emphasis is given to style in the typical real estate broker's presentation of individual houses. In this regard, the tract builder is due more credit, because the good ones give considerable thought to style elements and how they will appeal to buyers.

What, after all, is style? Style is an identity or personality—a manner, a look, usually representative in varying degrees of a region or of a period in time.

Obviously style has to involve continuity. If you dressed in threadbare blue jeans, a tuxedo shirt and an English bowler, you might be camp, but you would not be dressed in style. Yet, blue jeans, a bunchy turtleneck sweater, ankle boots and minimal but correct accessories impart a certain "style." Continuity, or a certain harmony between the various elements, has achieved this.

These days we refer to a "life-style" when we mean to identify a pattern or manner of living. This is a combination of level of income, a taste in friends, travel, recreational activity, reading, music, food, entertainment, an attitude about possessions or lack of them, clothing, autos, manner of speech and deportment, etc.

The collection of these and many other things makes up a recognizable continuity. Well-grooved life-styles give rise to handy labels such as "Florentine Humanism," or "Greenwich Village," or "Bauhaus," or "New York."

In the creation of housing, the architect, designer or builder generally strives for the inclusion of style elements, not only to give the house a personality of its own, but also to make it attractive to buyers and owners. The degree to which they achieve continuity or harmony is the measure of their success. It is more important than the elements themselves. The reason is that skillfully conceived, homogeneous, symmetrical or balanced lines and design elements create a blend that is both visually pleasing and durable.

What to Tell the Broker about the Style You Want

Catchword designations of traditional or classic house designs present a confusing starting point as a description to give a broker. For instance, to say you want a French Provincial or a Cape Cod or a Spanish house or the like is unnecessarily restricting to a broker unless you are looking in an area that abounds with that certain identifiable type of house.

As a house hunter, you are better off saying you want a house of traditional design as opposed to modern. You should emphasize consistency of design elements relative to the period. In actual practice, the French Country look is barely distinguishable from the English Country look of the same approximate period in history, especially when you consider that the builder is probably only including a smattering of the truly original design elements in his contemporary rendering of these styles. It is therefore better to relate to materials and textures and design "feel" than to these misleading handles.

Nevertheless, to help you build up a background of knowledge in basic, traditional, house-design elements, and to enable you better to identify houses in a particular style, the following drawings and descriptions are presented.

AMERICAN STYLES

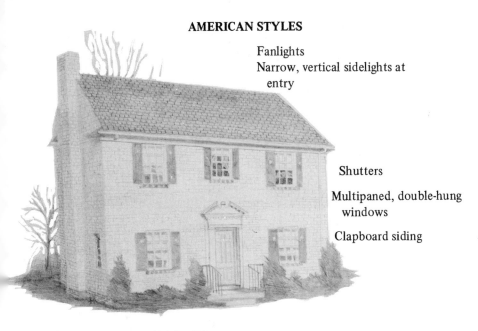

Fanlights
Narrow, vertical sidelights at
    entry

Shutters

Multipaned, double-hung
    windows

Clapboard siding

EARLY AMERICAN COLONIAL

Wood casement windows,
    double-hung sash later
Dormer windows
Gabled roof

Centrally placed, low, heavy
    chimney

CAPE COD

Gabled roof continue
   downward
(Gambrel roof also)
Wood siding

NEW ENGLAND SALTBOX

Clapboard siding
Projecting second story
Turned drops under projection
Casement windows

DUTCH COLONIAL

Multipaned double-hung windows

Thick walls of grey stone

PENNSYLVANIA DUTCH OR GERMAN

Projecting entry canopy
Shutters
Covered breezeway

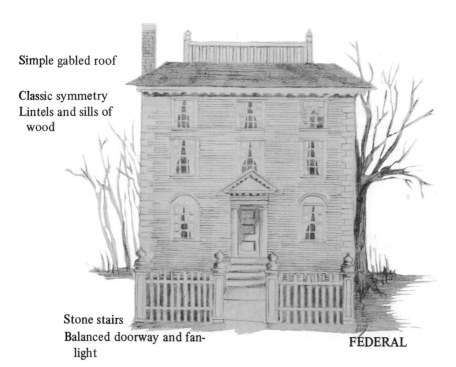

Simple gabled roof

Classic symmetry
Lintels and sills of
  wood

Stone stairs
Balanced doorway and fan-
  light

FEDERAL

Two-story columned veranda
Twin chimneys
Balustrade at roofline

Clapboard siding

Double-hung windows, long
shutters

SOUTH COLONIAL (MT. VERNON)

Two-story columns
Greek and Roman influence

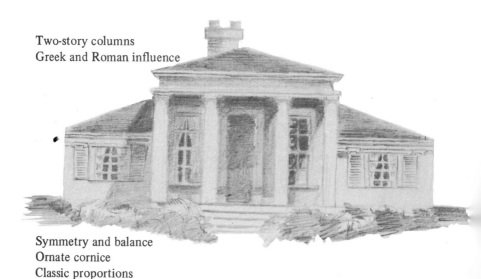

Symmetry and balance
Ornate cornice
Classic proportions

GREEK REVIVAL

ENGLISH STYLES

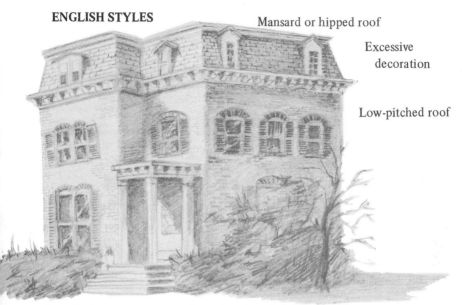

Mansard or hipped roof

Excessive
decoration

Low-pitched roof

Complexity
Wood ornamentation

Bays, turnings, balconied
towers

VICTORIAN

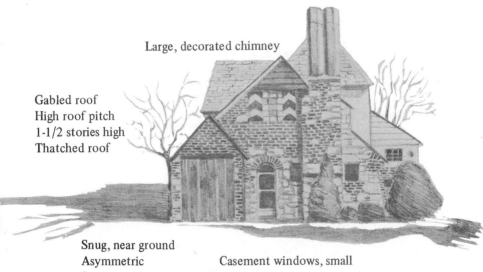

Large, decorated chimney

Gabled roof
High roof pitch
1-1/2 stories high
Thatched roof

Snug, near ground
Asymmetric
Stone quoins at corners

Casement windows, small
panes

COTSWOLD

Steep gables, complex roofline
Chimney pots
Low eaves, high chimney

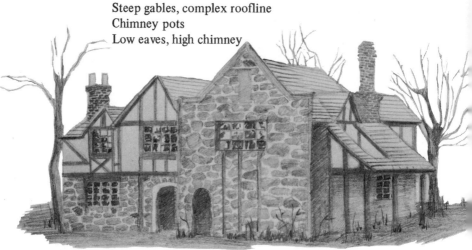

Stone and brick dominate   Imposing—2-1/2 stories
Some stucco and half-timbering Stone moldings (frames,
Leaded diamond windows   doors and windows)   TUDOR

Half-timber supports and
    stucco
Second-story overhang
Casement windows
Dormers
Bedrooms on second floor

ELIZABETHAN   Less stone and brick than
                                    Tudor

Classic cornice or eave (dentils)
Elongated French doors with
  shutters to ground

Double-hung windows
Twin symmetrical chimneys

Pediments
Quoins at corners
Hipped or gabled
  roof

GEORGIAN

Delicate iron grillwork
Bay windows with curving
  copper roof

Low-pitched, hipped roof

Simpler, less formal than
  Georgian
Stucco or brick

Octagonal windows above
  entry
Symmetrical facade, simple
  chimney

REGENCY

FRENCH STYLES

Stucco walls
Steep, curving roof
Casement windows
Prominent chimney

FARMHOUSE

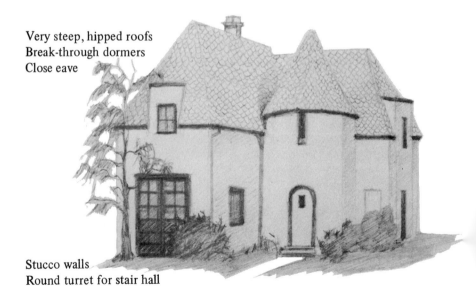

Very steep, hipped roofs
Break-through dormers
Close eave

Stucco walls
Round turret for stair hall

NORMANDY

Shingle roof
Broken cornice

Arched doorways, window
openings

FRENCH PROVINCIAL

Long windows with false sills
Brick, stone, or stucco
Quoin effect
Dentils

ITALIAN STYLES

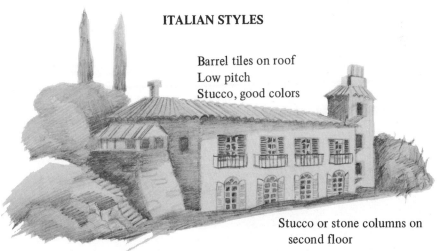

Barrel tiles on roof
Low pitch
Stucco, good colors

Stucco or stone columns on
second floor

Symmetry in windows and
doors
Strong classical influence

FLORENTINE

OTHER STYLES

Tilt-out shutters

Short roof spans
Tile slab roof covered with
  cement
Prominent chimney

Buttresses
Stucco walls

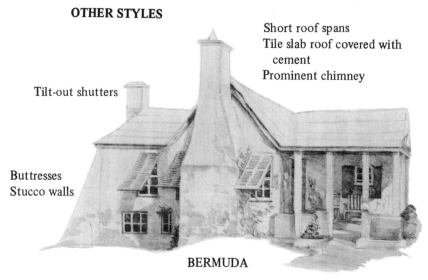

BERMUDA

Second-story windows with
long shutters, false sills

Unsupported, full-width
  balconies
Iron grillwork, columns,
  brackets

CREOLE—NEW ORLEANS

Long, unsupported balconies,
   wood balconies and railings
   and posts
Heavy shakes

Adobe or soft bricks on first
   floor
Batt-and-board sometimes on
   second floor

MONTEREY–MEXICAN COLONIAL

Recessed windows, doors
Minimum ornamentation
Wrought-iron grills, balconies
Stucco

Barrel tile
Low roof pitch

SPANISH STYLE

Little ornamentation

Low roof pitch

Functional but still much
emphasis on form   MODERN STYLE
Often plain or tractlike

Overhangs
Rich, natural texture,   Architect almost a necessity
  natural materials   No ornamentation
Low-pitched or flat roof   Creativity of design

Large areas of glass
Emphasis on function

CONTEMPORARY STYLE

Space frame
Cubes in space—creative
Large areas of glass
Flat roof

BAUHAUS

10
THE REALITIES OF MODIFIED STYLES

Modified Traditional Houses—And Why They Are There

It is a rare home that possesses *all* of the characteristics of a traditional, classic dwelling—all faithfully reproduced and maintained through the years. Therefore, in your house hunting, you can generally expect to find only modified versions of classic authenticity.

There are some practical reasons for this. In exterior walls, for example, stone and brick are expensive materials when used to build solid walls; therefore, walls are usually veneered with brick over ordinary stud framing, and often this effect is maintained only on the principal street elevation of the house. Also, stone casement frames for window openings and stone door jambs are almost unobtainable, unless an old house is being demolished and the builder can manage to scavenge these rarities. If they had to be made, a gravestone or tombstone mason would have to be employed at who-knows-what cost. Steep and complex roofs with numerous dormer windows and valleys are expensive to build and maintain. Copper for gutters and downspouts, and for bay-window roofs and flashing, has become almost prohibitive in cost. Slate is terribly expensive. Millwork required for special oversized cornices, curved windows and door openings, columns, dados, decorative ceiling moldings, casings, and base are frightfully dear these days even in softwood, and almost prohibitive in hardwoods like oak or walnut. Leaded glass, richly decorated iron grillwork, wood turnings, stair railings and balusters, cupolas, exterior moldings around windows and doors, even good half-timber work (still only an imitation of the actual structural timber framing showing in old Tudor houses), are all expensive items on today's building market.

Moreover, even if all of the materials were available at a reasonable cost, and there were workmen around to install them at fair prices, who would design their use? Few architects are available who possess the background to design such houses. Those who exist are more often than not engaged in some area of their profession that is more rewarding and challenging than custom residential architecture.

What Do Traditional and Good Modern Houses Have in Common?

What do you see when you first look at the exterior of a house?
1. The facade—that is, the front of it.
2. The roof—the top of it.
3. The fenestration—the door and window openings in
   it.

Your first impression of that *facade* is the very impression *your* buyer will receive when you are trying to sell the home some years from now. Bear in mind that unless you plan extensive remodeling, it will likely remain pretty much the same as you see it now. Therefore, you are buying this permanent impression and mortgaging yourself to the hilt to do it.

The *roof,* the generosity of its eaves and overhangs, its ultimate crowning of the facade, also makes up much of what your eyes are attracted to. Your attention begins there much as at a person's hat or his eyes. In contemporary houses the roof may be relatively flat, but it still should make some kind of a correlating statement, by the width or character of its facias (edge board), perhaps by some differing horizontal planes, or by its protective overhangs, its offering of shelter. Study the roof, and have confidence that it is proportioned correctly and that it makes its proper contribution to the overall effect.

The *fenestration* refers to the composition of door and window openings in the dwelling. Symmetry or intentional asymmetry are both legitimate tools in creating pleasing openings. However, be alert to the fact that many building designers and many more custom builders turning out their own designs are virtually unlettered in classical architectural principles. They are usually structurally and functionally oriented, but they have not learned how to make that delicate marriage of functionalism and beauty.

There is no written law that says that all windows *have* to be the same size or that their heads and sills *have* to line up exactly, or that they *have* to be defined by moldings around their edges. However, there is doubtless a law of architectural order somewhere opposing their all being of *different* sizes. The point should be obvious. Proportion, spacing, scale, trim, and that all-encompassing talent of good judgment is essential to the art of good residential design. As surely as you can judge the even spacing of place mats at a luncheon table or the grouping of pictures on a wall, you should be able to sense a satisfying balance in a facade due to good roof composition and a pleasing placement of door and window openings.

Buying What Cannot Be Replaced

We have described previously the appreciation aspects of the land itself, but there is also present an appreciation factor in certain types of houses. This refers to those houses that are too expensive to reproduce in today's building market. Whether due to the costliness of materials like stone, slate, choice metals, or hardwoods, or to the lack of trained artisans to work with these materials, certain fine, traditional houses and well-conceived contemporary houses can now only be built by the very rich and are usually out of the average house hunter's realm.

There do exist, however, traditional and modern houses of exceptional design, materials and workmanship such as the Tudor brick houses built in the 1920s and 1930s, the New England designs of someone like Royal Barry Wills, and the Frank Lloyd Wright-derived residences built in the 1930s and 1940s, not to mention the numerous custom homes done by talented architects for demanding and discriminating clients over the years. These houses, when they do come on the market, usually sell for prices considerably under their replacement costs—setting the land value aside.

If these residences have been correctly maintained, they generally make fine investments. Even the fussy, out-of-date Victorian house with its overornamented carpenter-Gothic styling is highly prized if it has been well executed and remains authentic, particularly in places like San Francisco where there remain many fine examples of this type.

This is not to say that oversized, run-down antique houses are always a good buy. Do not confuse irreplaceable features with obsolescence and loss of popularity. Be certain that your prize house has graduated or can graduate to the status of valuable antique and not simply be a white elephant. Great caution is required. Land location, as always, is the best overriding criterion.

Consistency with the Area

Be vitally aware of what is established and popular in a particular neighborhood. Do not succumb to the only contemporary house in a forest of stone Pennsylvania Dutch farmhouses. It was obviously built by an owner who did not want to conform, but why should you spend months searching for a similar free spirit when you try to sell the house? Even if it appears to be a bargain, will you be able to sell it easily? Will it appreciate?

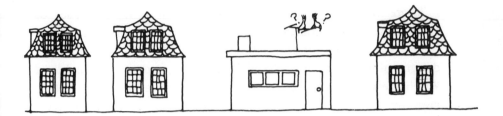

Just as in the case of buying the less grand property surrounded by better properties, try to find a house of the type that is popular in the area where you are looking that is priced under its neighbors. Then by cleverly decorating it, landscaping it and diligently maintaining it, you will have an excellent investment for the future.

11
WHICH WAY TO FACE? THE MATTER OF ORIENTATION

Orientation to the Sun

In fifteenth-century England, the Black Death had started in the south and worked its way northward. This created the notion that the plague was borne on the south wind. Fortunately for us, both the plague and the fear of the southern exposure have vanished. In fact, the more usable daytime rooms that can face the south, the better. This subject of sun orientation in your prospective home is of primary importance in enjoying the room arrangement within it.

The largest windows and patio sliding-door openings should ideally be facing south, with smaller openings in the other directions. The kitchen windows would be perfectly situated if they faced southeast, for they would then receive the cheering morning sun, and sun throughout most of the rest of the day. As we discuss later, in Chapter 13, the sun can play a vital role in the enjoyment of the individual rooms within the house, particularly during the six colder months from October to April.

The setting western sun presents a different kind of problem, and it is a specific threat to any room that might be utilized during the late hours of the afternoon. It does not harm bedrooms too

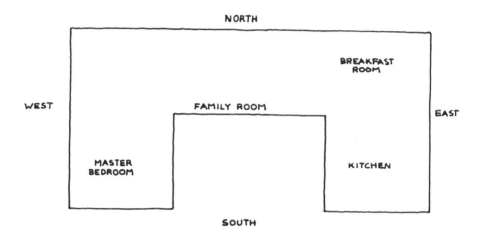

much, but it is unpleasant to endure in living, study and work areas. Guard against it, or you may find yourself imprisoned within a dark, curtained cell.

Remember that it is not enough just to have a long southerly house exposure if the right rooms are not actually faced that way. The rooms most depended upon for daytime living, such as the living room, family room, den, kitchen, auxiliary eating areas, should capitalize on a southerly exposure, and they will benefit from it. A whole line of bedrooms facing south, with these other rooms on the shady north side of the house, is an utter waste of precious sunlight. Admittedly that is sometimes the only way to lay out a house on certain sides of some neighborhood streets, but let that remain the seller's problem: do not bail him out of it.

Wind Orientation

Become aware of the direction of the *prevailing wind*. Then consider how it may benefit or harm your enjoyment of the house. If all outside living areas lay themselves open to this wind, you may be asking for trouble. Sometimes a hedge, a wall or a break in the terrain is sufficient to shield the patio in question, but satisfy yourself that this is the case.

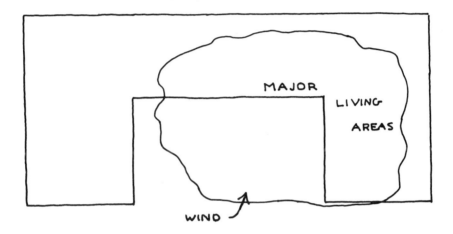

Maintaining the Property

A lot that is too large will entail a great deal of yard work, which, unless you or your family thrive on such activity, may prove to be a real burden. Someone has to take care of large lawns, flower beds, weeds, hedges, trees and even uncultivated areas where weeds and scrub can get started. So be mindful of tackling too much of an agricultural operation if you are not suited for it.

Examine the *steepness of the site.* If the terrain is too hilly or sloping, it makes maintenance even more of a chore because of the difficulty of walking about, the operation of any mechanical equipment, and even wheeling off cuttings and leaves by hand. Such a site may look attractive because of the views and the setting afforded the house, but project yourself into the future and visualize how you will be maintaining the property months and years from now. Furthermore, call to mind the resale problem that such a site may represent. Not everybody is a green-thumb artist or is able to afford a gardener.

House Orientation to Public View

No matter what size the lot may be, unless it is in the country or of estate-sized proportions, it is generally better to have a lot that is as wide as possible on the street side. This allows the home to make a better presentation toward the street, more or less showing a pleasant, longish facade as one approaches it. Moreover, the house wants to be situated so that outside recreation or work areas are shielded from public view. Otherwise, the largest and most inviting of outdoor patios will not be used since they are not private. One is apt to feel self-conscious about using such facilities. This can curb your maximum use and enjoyment of the property.

Rather an ideal setup is to have a wide lot fronting on the street to the north with one long side of the house, while the other long side, including all of the active living areas, their sliding doors, and patios, faces the south.

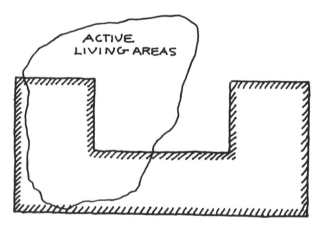

STREET

Alleys

A big advantage in older neighborhoods is an alley at the rear of residential property. If an alley is wide enough, the garages of the houses usually give onto them, greatly improving the appearance of the houses from the regular street, since driveways and open garage doors (or carports) are not visible. This also affords a great saving of space by eliminating the long driveway surface, which can be used for little else than the shuttling of cars to and fro.

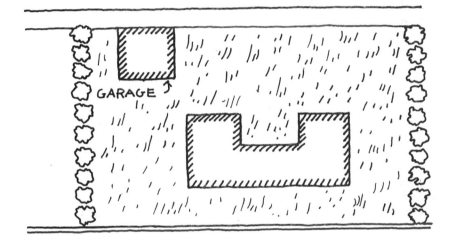

Trash pickups are usually handled from the alley, which avoids displaying unsightly trash cans two or three days a week. Additionally, utilities can enter from the alleys and be maintained out of sight of the street. Power poles, while unsightly, are at least less noticeable if they are run down an alley rather than directly in front of the houses on the street.

Driveways

Be sure that the driveway is negotiable by an average driver. Many house sales have been lost when it was discovered that the driveway layout was difficult or dangerous. Often this is something that cannot be changed, particularly in hilly areas where the driveway is winding and the turnaround space limited.

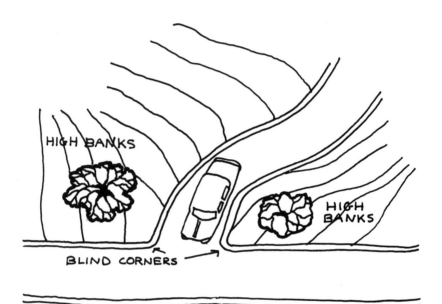

Driveways giving onto busy streets are singularly objectionable. If they are blind driveways, such as those that have steep banks right next to the street approach, vision may be impaired in one or both directions. Such a setup is an invitation to suicide. Also, driveways that are too steep are hazardous because of the danger of a car getting out of control and whizzing down it, endangering all in its path. Bear in mind what the driveway will be like with snow and ice on it, or on a rainy day.

Here is a driveway checklist to help you avoid a difficult predicament yourself and to avoid a sluggish resale problem if you are tempted to get entangled:

1. Driveway should be negotiable by average-to-timid driver.
2. Driveway should have more than ample turnaround room for larger-than-average car.
3. Driveway should not give onto busy street, particularly if you have to back onto street.
4. Driveway should not have blind approach(es) to street, even if you drive into street head on.
5. Driveway should not be too steep (greater than a 12 percent slope).
6. Driveway should be negotiable in winter.

12
EXTERIOR SETTING, TERRAIN AND DRAINAGE

Landscaping and Trees—Their Valuable Contribution

The landscaping on a property can be a substantial but very often overlooked asset in establishing the true value of a house under consideration. It is almost always "thrown in" without evaluation by either the seller or the buyer, although under certain conditions it looms as a large asset in any comprehensive appraisal of the offering. Well-organized, well-managed landscaping with good irrigation and good drainage is a very real plus and can be assigned a value right along with extra fireplaces, oversized water heaters and one-piece toilets.

This is not to say that a jungle of blue gum eucalyptus, a thicket of podocarpus and an old yellow lawn with lumpy bald spots of hard earth showing is worth anything at all. It is not. On the contrary. As a matter of fact, such jungles represent a *minus* quantity because of the immense cost of removing them or cutting them back and replacing them.

In buying a tract or subdivision house, eschew the landscaping that the builder may offer to put in for you. Accept, instead, the allowance that is usually given as an alternative. The reason is that the landscaping he normally puts in is of the type that is intended to instantly "bush up" the place. It is not chosen with an eye to what it will look like five years from now; rather, it is usually cheap, large or fast growing, anything for immediate effect. Take the allowance, small as it is, and select small but precisely chosen plants and shrubs and place them with an eye for maximum visual effect. You will know that in years to come the mature landscaping will better suit the property than what the builder would have used for dramatic sales appeal.

Remember to upgrade your evaluation of a house that has good, mature landscaping, terracing, irrigation and drainage; downgrade it if it has minimal planting or much that needs to be torn out and replaced.

Swimming Pools

There must be a law of practicality somewhere to the effect that the amount of swimming pool use varies in inverse proportion

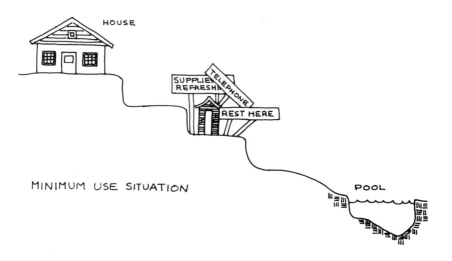

to its nearness to the residence. Do not be intrigued with lovely terraces cascading down (or up) to a swimming pool, where the broker points out what a lovely setting it occupies and what a nice view you have of it from the house, or vice versa. As the months wear on, this type of remote pool orientation wears as thin as a hillside garage, where you have to hike up a flight of stairs with armloads of groceries.

For maximum use and enjoyment, the pool should be rather near to the house, sheltered from the prevailing wind, and not overshadowed by large trees, which create the problem of excessive shade and too many falling leaves.

Examine the pool equipment and find out about its age and method of upkeep. Automatic pool-cleaning devices have taken much of the tedium and expense out of pool maintenance. Sweeping devices save the most labor, with those that add chemicals automatically running a close second. So if the pool lacks such equipment, study the possibility of adapting it in the future so that these maintenance cares do not become a noose around your neck.

Drainage—A Thorough Check

Rainwater must not only be collected from the roof of the house and led away from its foundation perimeter, but it must also be led from the property along with *all* the water that falls onto the property that doesn't sink into the ground. This is called the "runoff." This surface water is a matter that warrants serious attention. Most home buyers satisfy themselves that the roof appears to have adequate drainage and proceed no further in their exploration of what actually happens to the roof water and the surface water.

Sandy soil will usually absorb reasonable amounts of runoff water either descending onto its surface or poured onto it from the roof or other areas. However, soil that is high in clay content with the typical layer of "hard pan" beneath the surface will only absorb water up to a point. Then the surface water must find someplace else to go.

It would be ideal if you could visit the prospective property in a heavy downpour and really see where the water goes. Even immediately following a good storm, it is informative to visit the property and look for those routes taken by excessive runoff. These are generally quite easily detectable.

Often driveways, walks, patios and pool decks do not drain properly, and water stands until it evaporates—which may be a matter of days—or until it is sponged up or squeegeed off. Do not be embarrassed to ask if you can turn on a hose to see if such suspect areas drain properly. You might still want the house if it did not have good surface drainage, but you would then have your eyes open to the problem and might even negotiate a lower price based upon your estimated expense to eliminate the problem.

Follow this sequential procedure in checking for adequate water drainage:

1. Examine the general roof layout and satisfy yourself that it appears to drain satisfactorily and logically within the roof area itself.

a. Note attentively any roof section that drains onto another roof to see if this surcharge of extra water can be handled properly.

b. Note any flat or near-flat area to determine how it might drain.

2. Go over the gutter and downspout arrangement and satisfy yourself that it "reads." That is, ascertain that one drainage function follows the other in logical sequence.

3. Observe the manner in which water is collected from the downspouts (called the "collection system"), how this roof water relates to the rest of the property, and how it is disposed of.

4. Check concrete areas such as patios, driveways, pool decks, walks, to see that area drains or catch basins are present or that sloping surfaces drain in a logical manner—away from the house.

5. In landscaped areas look for ruts, holes, freshwater gouging, puddling, etc., to satisfy yourself that excessive surface water runoff has routes available to move expediently off of the property.

6. Relate roof areas, concrete areas, and landscaped areas in a comprehensive search for the answer to this question: In an extreme storm condition, how does the excess water from all three of these sources leave the property to proper streets, alleys or storm drains?

7. Lastly, cast your eyes onto adjacent properties and be sure that your prospective house is not vulnerable to receiving the runoff of any other adjacent property.

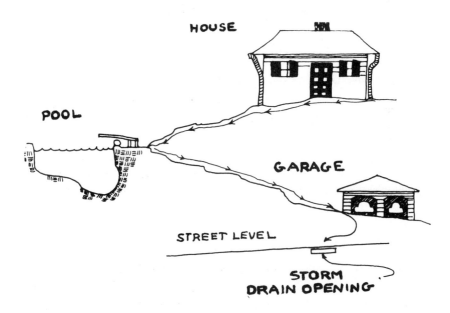

Be sure in checking area drains and catch basins that you understand the difference between those interconnected to a true water collection and drainage system and those merely spilling out into the open ground or giving into "drywells" or sumps. These latter devices are usually added after a surfaced concrete area is found to drain poorly and the owner wishes to avoid the cost of revamping the area. A hole is simply cut in the lowest sections where the water tends to puddle. The hole is filled with gravel and a grill put over the opening.

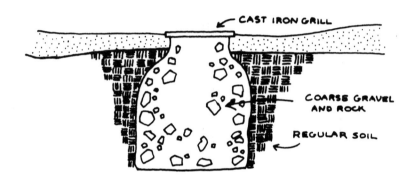

Depending on their size, these drywells or sumps work satisfactorily for a while but have two major weaknesses:

1. They eventually silt up and must be reexcavated and have fresh gravel added.

2. They are unable to handle large amounts of water, since they can only drain as rapidly as the soil surrounding the gravel-filled cavity accepts the water.

Pumping Devices

Occasionally, pumps are needed in areas that will not drain without mechanical assistance. This includes basements and garages below grade. These pumps are activated by a solonoid that floats; when a certain level of water is reached, the pump is switched on.

Explore such devices in great detail. Ask for an explanation by the seller to determine if you feel content about this problem.

These "sump pumps" behave with less temperament when activated once a month or so by temporary flooding with a hose. You might try this as a test of the vitality of the pump if you are considering a house with any such drainage aid.

13
FLOOR-PLAN BASICS

There has been much written about good and bad floor plans, whether there is proper traffic circulation instead of having to walk through one room in order to get to another, etc. Here are some good, basic points to take note of in checking out the floor plan of a house.

—An entry way that *fits the scale* of the total residence.

—Pleasant ascending or descending stairs that are not mean.

—Plenty of sunlight available to those rooms most used for daytime living.

—Entry that does not go directly from the front door into the living room.

—A living room that does not serve as a hallway to another room.

—A dining room or area that is separate enough to have its own personality and "feel."

—An adequate, modern kitchen plus a secondary eating area for breakfast, short luncheons or snacks.

—A family room, recreation room, activity room, playroom, den or library or office—that is, some place to be *besides* the living room or bedroom.

—Required number of bedrooms, baths and closets, with a powder room for guests.

—Auxiliary entrances to hard-used areas of the house such as family room or breakfast room.

—A garage that is easy to get to from service areas such as the back porch and kitchen.

—Easy disposal of trash and garbage.

—Simple, direct traffic pattern between heavy linen-use areas and washer/dryer.

—Ability of heads of house to function within the master bedroom area without needing the rest of the house; includes the use of a "suite" arrangement or an office within master bedroom area.

While frightfully generalized, to a greater or lesser extent these requirements seem to summarize what many buyers seem to be looking for in floor plans and circulation. The floor plans by which these criteria are achieved are infinite, but the need for checking any plans offered against these guidelines *plus* your own personal preferences is obvious.

What Are Standard Room Sizes?

The sizes of ideal rooms is clearly a subjective matter; however, here are some suggested, somewhat typical room sizes for checking against your house finds:

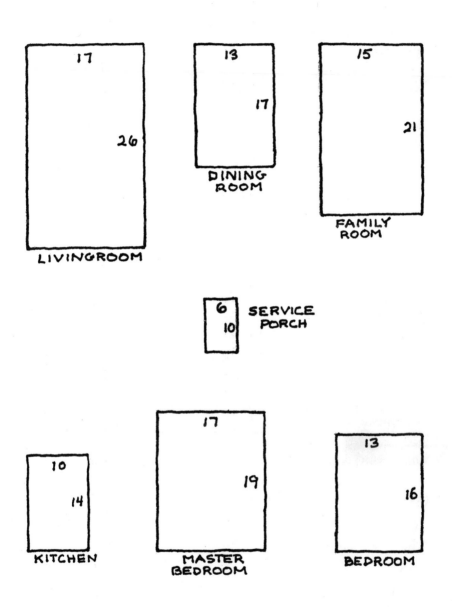

17

26

LIVINGROOM

13

17

DINING
ROOM

15

21

FAMILY
ROOM

6

10

SERVICE
PORCH

10

14

KITCHEN

17

19

MASTER
BEDROOM

13

16

BEDROOM

Split-Level Houses

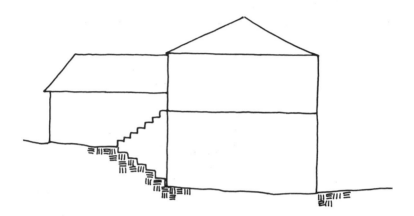

The split-level home has achieved a high degree of popularity in the United States. This concept enables the builder to utilize rolling terrain without adhering strictly to level pad sites and to come up with many pleasing 1-1/2-story facades that make a nice presentation to the street for sales purposes. Additionally, split-levels have an apparent advantage as a compromise over the two-story, since movement from one level to the next is made by only half flights of stairs.

One disadvantage of split-levels for smallish families would seem to be the disorientation of living room to the family room. That is, there is an inability in some split-level designs to have a smooth visual and traffic flow through all living areas of the house, not a problem in the traditional two-story house or the one-story ranch or modern house. You just have to decide if this lack of visual and traffic continuity in the hard-used living areas is desirable or undesirable and stick with the decision.

Converting a Bedroom into a Den

Many people make the mistake of looking at houses that have no more than their exact bedroom requirements. This limits resale potential and the possibility of acquiring an extra usable room.

If there is an extra bedroom in the house you are buying, or if the family outgrows its use, converting it into a den seems to be the natural thing to do. The only trouble is that the forsaken bedroom is seldom located out of the general traffic pattern enough to make it an ideal retreat. One solution is to isolate it from sound as much as possible by a solid wood door, to give it its own source of music, and then to replace a window with a sliding glass door or French doors giving onto a small walled-off garden of its own. These changes would give it as much separation as possible.

Few would dispute the value of concentration, meaning *private* concentration as a vital factor in fruitful living. If there is a regular den or library in conjunction with the general living rooms of the house, that is very nice, but the idea of a private retreat may be violated if it flows too directly from those rooms used for family living. The presence of a small cubbyhole, perhaps situated off or near the master bedroom, is the ideal location for the man or woman of the house to withdraw to for moments of thoughtfulness, reading, study or listening quietly to music.

The Home as an Office

According to Pierre Dufan, chief architect of civil buildings and national palaces in France, the home of the future will be playing a much larger role than it does at present. The family dwelling will be the place where more time is spent than any other place. By the year 2000, as the world moves away from a factory-oriented to a paper-oriented society, much more work will be done at home. What a fine additional reason for a small private office or stury, when one considers not only its present possible uses, but the resale implications for the prospective buyer of the future.

It is not frivolous to think that those special little features of a floor plan, such as a precious, sunny, southeast breakfast room and a snug, private den, that so much intrigue you, the current buyer, will attract the next person to the house as well.

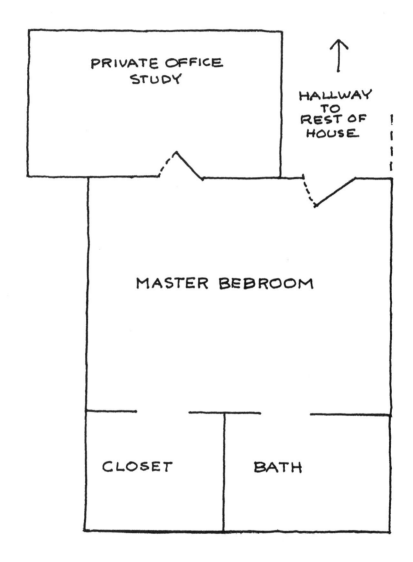

Sun—Its Relationship to the House Interior

It would be ideal if, as one progressed through the day, the sun were available to warm an elbow or a back, glint off breakfast silver and luncheon dishes and glasses, warm and air musty beds at just the right time when they are first turned back in the morning, make the living room inviting in the mornings and afternoons when they are otherwise deserted, and cast warming rays on the family-room tiles and on the kitchen sink and counters.

During the warm summer months, when the sun is almost directly overhead in traversing its east-west pattern, and when most windows usually have adequate sunlight available, this presents no particular problem. In your house-hunting, though, imagine the months of late fall, winter and early spring, and visualize what windows and sliding doors the sun will enter when it assumes its low, southerly angle.

Since all rooms cannot have the morning sun, a priority would surely be the kitchen and breakfast areas where the morning activities are at their early peak. Southeast is the best exposure for kitchen and breakfast room. If several bedrooms could have morning sun as well, it would be very freshening. Later in the afternoon, the family room, living room and private den or office would be nice places to receive a shaft of sunlight in order to make them inviting and attractive to be in. Some windows and doors can be enlarged fairly easily and inexpensively to let in more sun, but only the floor plan can assure the potentiality of rooms that are gifted with this cheering and salutary benefit.

Make this "sun search" part of your house-hunting program, and make a sketch like the one on the following page to help you visualize the rooms affected.

Unorthodoxy

Sometimes the "bright ideas" of an owner are valuable assets, such as increased and well-designed cabinet and storage spaces,

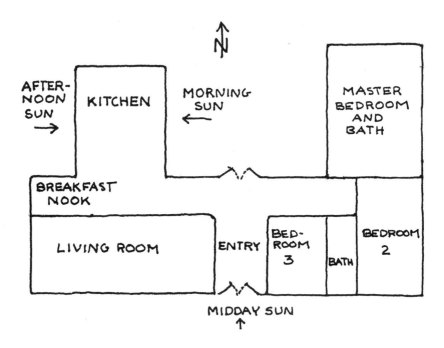

certain labor-saving appliances that are built in, better-quality hardware, doors, lighting, and, of course, all elements of beauty and functionalism that have stood up to some tests of experience and worthiness.

However, some "bright ideas" consist of such things as entirely open floor plans (walls not extended to ceiling height), glass partitions between rooms, niches instead of separate rooms for toilets or whole bathrooms, unusual materials as yet unproven or *accepted by the public,* exposed structural elements like trusses, exposed bracing, bars, straps, etc., concealed fluorescent lighting in living and dining rooms, and all other like gimcrackery. If the real estate marketplace spoke, it would chuckle and then perhaps groan when the houses with the glass-brick wall (remember?) or the radiant-heated ceiling that looked like the bottoms of egg crates (remember?) or the all-black plumbing fixtures (remember?), the imitation brick, the conversation pit, overornate ironwork, come onto the market. These "bright idea" houses require special buyers, and if you remain intent on seeing your house purchase grow into a good investment, leave these monuments to the expression of personal ids for the kindred "free spirit" that will someday surface and take the seller out of his misery. *Shun unorthodoxy!*

14
OTHER
FLOOR-PLAN IDEAS

The Importance of Alternative Eating Areas

Ideally, there would be a breakfast area in or near the kitchen, also getting a good dose of morning sun. Not only breakfast but frequently luncheon is enjoyable in areas of the house other than in the main dining room. Then, in the family or recreation room or adjacent patio, balcony or terrace, there would also be an area for possible use at luncheon or dinner on warm days. Lastly, there would naturally be the regular dining room or separated dining area for some midday dining and particularly for dinner meals.

The point is that these different locations give station and importance and variety to the different meals during the day. Breakfast, since it is usually a very simple, almost one-course affair, is hardly up to the significance of a separate, large, set-up room that is usually a bit too far from the kitchen and the starting-up activity of the early part of the day. Many furnished condominium models are reflecting this desire for diverse eating locations. It is not unusual in condominiums of 1,500 to 1,600 square feet to have a formal dining area, breakfast nook and balcony or patio set-up as well.

Are Closets Important? Yes, But . . . !

A good rule of thumb is that each adult should have about 8 to 10 feet of hanging space. Children can get along with a little less, but as they grow, of course, this requirement will enlarge. It would be ideal to have 10 feet per person. This is easy to work out, inasmuch as it comes to about four normal walking steps per person. If the house you are looking at has much less than this, be aware that you are making a compromise. However, if there are redeeming features, figure out how closet space might be increased by building additional space or by furnishing the shorted rooms with an armoire type of wardrobe—that is, a piece of furniture that resembles a small closet that is free standing. Really give a black mark to any room represented as a bedroom, or one that's *convertible* to a bedroom, that has no closet at all.

Basement, garage storage areas, storage closets, pantries, generous stand-up attics with good stairs up to them are all valuable assets. There is a great temptation when building houses for sale—so-called "spec" houses—to skimp on storage space. After all, storage space and closets are not glamorous elements to talk about once the builder has attained his "adequacy level." Such spaces must yield the spotlight to such things as natural wood cabinets, new-model built-in appliances, fireplaces, pools, patios, beams and more such magnetic features. Moreover, a spec house is empty of all belongings and so does not look at all cluttered.

Stairs—Looking at Them with a Critical Eye

Be wary of "mean" stairs. What are ideal stairs? They first of all have a good, comfortable "rise" and "run."

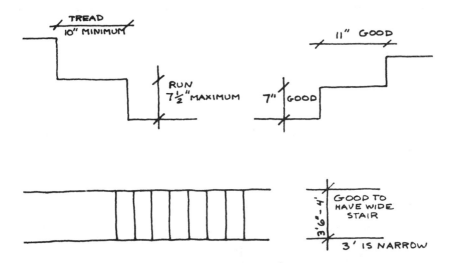

Stairs are easier to climb, safer and better looking when their ascension is broken with a landing, or even two landings. Straight runs of stairs are aesthetically unpleasing and sometimes dangerous because of the likelihood of someone falling down the whole flight, possibly hitting a wall or glass at the bottom.

Balusters (or "spindles") should be spaced 6 to 9 inches apart for safety, and the railing should be at least 36 inches high and tested for steadiness.

It is best if there is a second-floor landing running around part of the stair hall. This minimizes the starkness of too many full-height, two-story walls. One or two might be fine, but three sheer walls surrounding the stairwell makes for a shaftlike feeling if spaces are otherwise minimal. On the other hand, with second-

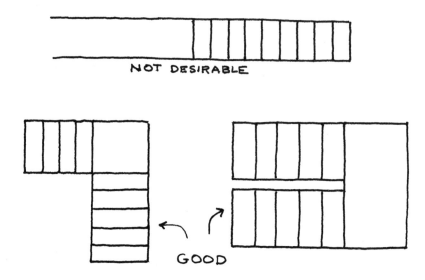

floor landings, the result of broken vertical lines is a gracious, beckoning effect that makes your ascent more inviting. This is further aired by generous amounts of natural daylight and good artificial lighting at night.

The role of an easy set of stairs and a gracious ground-floor foyer and upstairs stair hall in making a two-story home more delightful is grossly underestimated. Designers and builders sometimes begrudge this seeming waste of space, but they are shortsighted.

Here is a checklist to aid in your evaluation of the quality of stairs:

	BEST	GOOD	FAIR	WORST
Rise (vertical)	6½″	7″	7½″	8″
Run (horizontal)	12″	11″	10″	9″
Width of tread	4′	3′6″	3′	2′6″

	BEST	GOOD	FAIR	WORST
Railing	firm	slight vibration	vibration	wobbly
Baluster spacing	6″	8″	10″	12″
Number of landings	2	1	0	pie-shaped
Lighting—natural	excellent	good	fair	bad
Lighting—artificial	excellent	good	fair	bad
First-floor foyer	generous	adequate	skimpy	none
Second-floor stair hall	generous	adequate	skimpy	none
Two-story high walls	none	1	2	3

Basements

Many older homes and some new ones boast this old-fashioned, precious feature—the basement. There are some real advantages to this underground area:

—A convenient starting point for any under-floor repairs that may be necessary in the future.

—A storage facility.

—A necessity if heat and hot water are circulated by natural heat rise (thermal syphon) methods and not aided by mechanical pumps or fans.

—A wine cellar, if the heating units and water heater are compartmentalized.

If there is a basement, do not behave like some buyers and say, "Oh, that's all right" and not bother to check it out. Look at it! Much of the rough construction of the house is visible down there: the method of workmanship, underfloor electrical conduit, water pipes, water heating and heating units, etc. Also, it will help you visualize how you yourself might utilize this area to better advantage in the future.

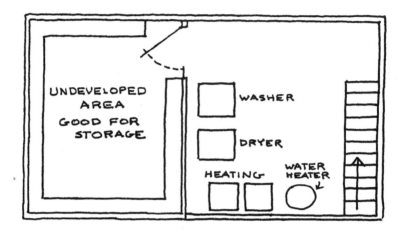

Water seepage into a basement is extremely difficult to curtail. As for detecting it, first attempt to sense any musty, damp, cellar odor. Then look for signs of powdery, greyish or brownish dust on the floor in telltale water patterns. Other clues are futile attempts at caulking the insides of the walls, or, of course, the conclusive presence of a sump pump or drywell.

To cure this, if one or more basement walls lines up with the first floor outside walls of the house above, chances are that a regrading of the outside yard to slope *away* from the house, firmly compacting the new soil by tamping it, and planting a dense, compact ground cover might stem the tide. The radical and thorough solution is to excavate the outside perimeter of the basement walls down to the footings and apply a double membrane of fiber glass and epoxy to the vertical surface so it becomes an immense reverse shower pan. Obviously, this costs money, so be forewarned.

Square Footage—Know the Size of the House

Do not accept prima facie the square footage given to you by an owner. Professional appraisers find that about one out of four homeowners honestly believes his house to be larger than it actually is, and that is the reason that the first thing they do is a measurement.

The broker's listing will show the square footage of living space in the house. If you are in doubt about it, satisfy yourself by totaling it up. Add up all of the living areas, including measurements to the *outsides* of all walls. This does not include the garage. A lender or appraiser will be interested in the total square footage and will add the garage, plus any decks, balconies or large overhangs. Usually he "weights" these secondary, nonliving areas by assigning the garage two-thirds of its square-foot area, and the decks and all about one-third. The total of all this provides the "net square footage" of the improvements. Cube footage is not generally referred to any longer.

Dimensions and Furniture Arrangement

A good practice, if the original plans for the home you are starting to get serious about are not available, is to make an actual drawing of the floor plan in 1/4-inch scale. An easy and very quick way to do this is to pace off the major perimeter dimensions of the house in this manner:

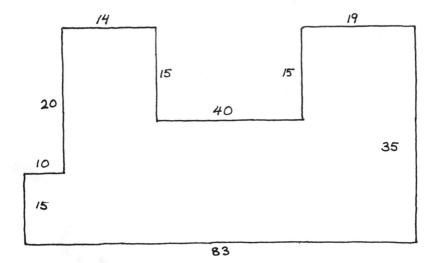

Then pace off dimensions of the principal rooms like the living room, dining room, family rooms, the master bedroom and kitchen. Later, at home, you can fill in the other rooms roughly enough for this purpose.

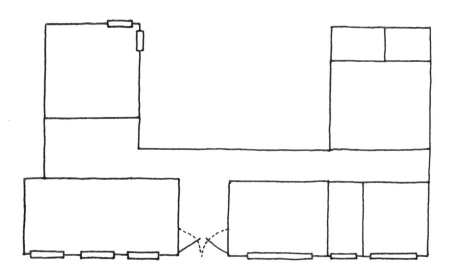

Then place the doors and windows as exactly as you can remember them. Last, you can draw in your present furniture and evaluate how well it can be utilized in the house and how traffic patterns will actually work. Also indicate the kitchen and service-porch cabinets and the various work areas outside of the house, and plot the course of traffic to and from all these areas. One of the most repeated trips is from the refrigerator to the kitchen sink and drainboard; if this distance is excessive you could be letting yourself in for a lot of traveling.

DESIRABLE

UNDESIRABLE

What about Remodeling?

Try to avoid the house that cannot be used without extensive structural remodeling. You seldom get your money out of a remodeling project. Decorating, on the other hand, frequently pays off. There is a lot of difference in expense, and of course if you remodel, you *still* are stuck with the decorating on top of it.

However, if remodeling is inevitable or obligatory, bear in mind that the cost of expanding horizontally on the first floor is dramatically less expensive than expanding on the second. Simple ground floor additions are the cheapest and most productive of remodeling projects because they create instant square footage *added to* the existing structure.

The cost per foot of Addition B would be about twice the cost of Addition A. The contractor has to figure in so much demolition and reconstruction work within the existing house. So, in examining floor plans, be sure you see an easy first-floor way to expand, if you have to do it at all.

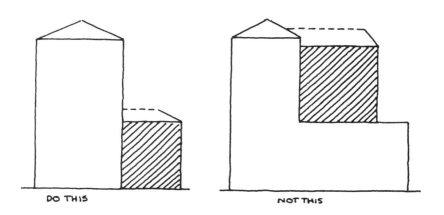

DO THIS   NOT THIS

15
LET'S TALK OF LUMBER AND THE HOUSE FRAME

Building Codes and Setbacks

In older neighborhoods, where lots are relatively small or where uses for multiple dwellings and light commercials are mixed in with single family homes, confine your house hunting to those areas where residential use is consistent. This can influence lenders and your future buyers. Many lenders and buyers shy away from free-zoning concepts. This tendency does not rule out neighborhoods that include scattered specialty shops, small markets or service stations, but it is aimed at a whole block of stores or light-manufacturing buildings on one side of the street and houses on the other.

Do some research to assure yourself that the house under consideration conforms to the setbacks and height limitations. If the garage is a separate building, this means checking it as well to see that it is not too near an alley or the side property lines. Matters of encroachment might show up on a preliminary title report, but encroachments into the city's required setbacks *within* the boundaries of your own lot would likely not show up.

Nothing much is done about long-standing setback violations. However, if you attempt to remodel, alter or rebuild a portion of the home, you could be prevented from doing this until you agree to rectify the encroachment. This can be costly. Such a condition would create a stumbling block in reselling the house, even if you did not contemplate remodeling during your ownership. Here are some other building code requirements that could be a problem:

—Insufficient garage spaces (usually two required per house). (Be on guard here for the prior conversion of one garage space for some use such as a playroom or a bedroom; it might have to be changed back.)

—Minimum garage space in current codes is 9 by 20 feet.

—Minimum ventilation in any room used for living: 1/8 of the square footage of the room in window space (half of that must open).

—Minimum ceiling height is usually 7 feet 6 inches.

—Access to all closed-off areas such as attics and space under house.

—Venting of attic and under-house space.

—Self-closing doors separating house from garage.

—Walls in common with garage to have fire-retardent plaster or drywall.

What Underflooring Is Best—Slab or Conventional Wood Frame?

Most new homes built on level ground are constructed with *concrete slab floors*. This drawing shows the relative complication in building up wood floors and why the builder prefers the slab:

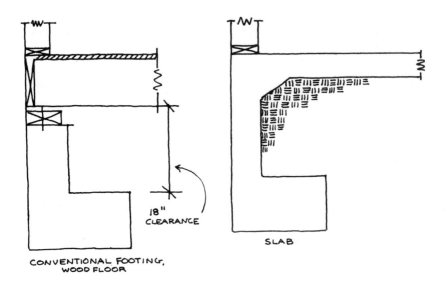

18"
CLEARANCE

SLAB

CONVENTIONAL FOOTING,
WOOD FLOOR

It costs the builder about fifty cents a square foot for the slab
floor and about seventy-five cents for a wood floor, exclusive of
any hardwood applied over the plywood "subfloor." Additionally,
the wood floor must be held high off the ground, which causes
aesthetic problems in designing relatively small houses on level lots
without providing generous porches or terraces. Vents, access, or
crawl holes must be provided to the underfloor areas. There is also
extra trouble and expense for the subtrades to fasten underground
installations of plumbing, electrical, and gas and heating to the
bottom of the joists rather than simply laying them in shallow
trenches.

Some people think the slab is warmer and less drafty, since it is
right on the ground. The counterargument is that the space between the ground and a wood floor actually can insulate the first
floor, much as an attic insulates the ceiling, particularly if it is
vented on all sides and sheathed with aluminum under the joists.

Some say the slab is rigid, that it makes no noise or squeaks. However, its very rigidity can be a disadvantage. The wood floor's slight springiness provides a more resilient surface to the point where people with chronic back problems will often demand wood floors for this very reason, stating that concrete floors aggravate their condition. Similarily, those with joint ailments such as arthritis often feel the dampness that is transmitted through the concrete.

Oak Hardwood Flooring or Masonry Flooring vs. Carpeting

From the buyer's standpoint, a really well-built house would have permanent floors of hardwood or masonry tile or brick, marble, terrazzo, etc. Wall-to-wall carpeting is not permanent flooring and must someday be replaced, maybe several times. Permanent flooring of wood or masonry represents an *extra* cost to the builder that is pretty much wasted in a spec house where he plans to cover a great deal of this permanent flooring with wall-to-wall carpeting.

Therefore, consider hardwood or masonry floors as a hallmark of good building practice. This is more significant in the "living" rooms of the house (living room, dining room, family room, den) than in the bedrooms, where the decoration lends itself more to full carpeting.

Foundations—Are They Sound?

Here are two ways to examine the house for any possible foundation deficiencies. First, look through the rooms on the inside and make a careful note of any large cracks in plastered walls. If the house is drywalled, any large, major settling will cause tension in the drywall sheet and will show a pattern of tension—as if the skeleton of a fish were concealed just under the surface. Be on the lookout for these fossillike ridges where the outer layer seems to be straining to hold the inner core together. Minor cracks like those that occur over door and window openings or diagonally at their upper corners are of no great concern. Generally, the *major* indications of substantial strain or settling are what you need to look for.

Any such large crack may still only mean some "differential" settling among the related flexible wood structural members of the house frame. However, the next step is to examine the perimeters of the house down near where the ground meets the foundation and ascertain if there is a vertical crack evident in the foundation. The idea is to define a crack as originating from foundation settling, not merely movements within the wood frame.

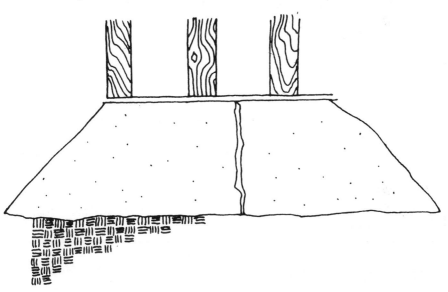

If a crack appeared over an inside foundation, called an intermediate foundation or footing, it will be necessary for someone to crawl under the house with a flashlight to the point under the interior wall.

A foundation crack is not the end of the world. Provided there is not more than one or that it is not a result of earth subsidence or slippage, they are not all that hard to remedy. A cut-through section of the repair would look as follows:

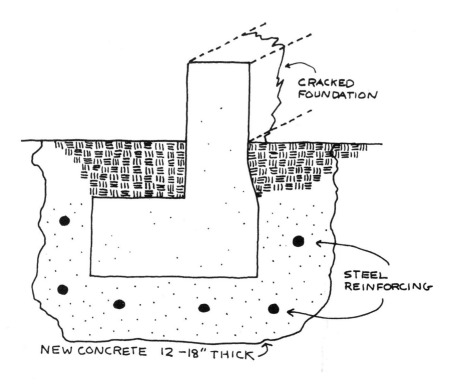

CRACKED FOUNDATION

STEEL REINFORCING

NEW CONCRETE 12 –18" THICK

Ceiling Heights

The standard ceiling height for residential construction is 8 feet. Almost all tract and subdivision houses are built with ceilings of this height. In larger rooms such as the living room, a good-sized dining room or family room, and certainly the stair hall or entry foyer, this height often seems oppressively low to even a person of average height. Imagine what it must feel like to an individual over 6 feet. It is particularly bad if any beams, whether real or false, have been used in the construction of the ceiling and they project down below the 8-foot height. The 8-foot minimum really should apply to the bottom of any beams.

Nine or, preferably, 10-foot ceilings are far more desirable, but they are not commonly found in new houses unless they are custom designed or executed by a far-thinking tract builder of better-quality tract homes.

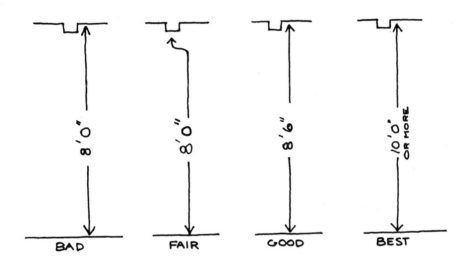

What Are Vapor Barriers?

Vapor barriers are important in many areas of the country where excessive dampness and humidity can cause a buildup of moisture and bacteria within the walls.

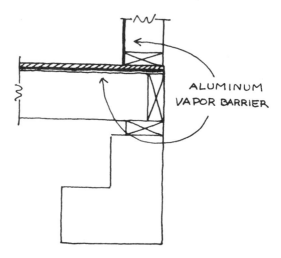

Of varying types and applications, the barrier amounts to an insulating shield of plastic or moistureproof paper usually installed on the interior side of wall studs and floor joists to prevent condensation. This insulation can be discovered by examining the material around a TV or electrical outlet in an outside wall or the underside of plywood subflooring. It is most essential in areas utilizing air-conditioning and heating to a degree that contrasts greatly with the environment.

Lumber Quality

Almost any area of the country utilizes some form of building code or manual that not only attempts to restrict the builder from building improperly and improvising, but aids him by specifying certain size materials for certain purposes. Rarely does a builder intentionally undersize the (main) structural members in a house. This is because the saving is so slight in comparison to the risk involved.

House hunters are sometimes guided down into the basement of an older home by the real estate agent and shown the large 4 by 14, 4 by 16 or 6 by 16 girders running under the floor joists.

"They don't build 'em like this anymore," he will intone, eyeing reverently a fat girder beneath the floor joists. This is nonsense. If the house has a built-up wood floor, the builder can support the subfloor in one of three ways:

1. Continuous concrete foundations and small floor joists.

2. Intermediate large girders (beams) breaking the span of all floor joists.

3. Large 2 by 10 or 2 by 12 floor joists requiring no girders and fewer intermediate footings.

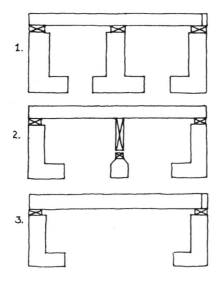

It is about six of one and half a dozen of the other which method is used. Often the footing-to-girder-to-joist arrangement is based on the first-floor wall layout and how it relates to the second floor and roof loads above it. Different parts of a wood floor may be designed utilizing all three of the support methods. For the builder to use unnecessarily large underpinnings is like wearing a belt and suspenders. Often this was done in the old days because the builder simply did not know the exact support members required and chose to be ultracareful.

What's in the Attic?

An inspection of the attic will reveal several things about the house:

—Quality of various sizes of lumber and appearance of rough carpentry.

—Adequacy of venting.

—Quality of roof, how supported, and if leaks are apparent.

16
OTHER ELEMENTS OF
THE HOUSE FRAME

Masonry—Fireplaces and Chimneys

It is hard to tell if a fireplace draws well without testing it, but a clue to its performance would be to examine the flues (roundish terra-cotta pipes) at the top of the chimney. This fireplace-to-flue relationship is a very critical one. By standing at a distance and looking up at the flue projection, you can often judge its size by comparison with others nearby. You can determine if it seems generous or not, a size of 13 by 17 inches being average. A large fireplace opening requires a very large flue. Building inspectors are more strict about this now, but previously they used to leave such matters up to the mason and builder, who often got away with the minimum they thought acceptable.

Check inside the fireplace to see if it has an operable damper. Just look up inside the opening and see if an iron handle projects down from above. With some newspaper or a rag protecting your hand from the soot, move the handle to see if it operates to close off the chimney. By restricting the loss of warm air up the chimney in cold weather, considerable savings can be made in heating the house.

If you would like to test a fireplace, be sure you do the following three things:

1. Be certain that the damper blade is in the *open* position.

2. In cold weather, place something readily combustible like crumpled newspaper or light kindling *on top* of the larger fireplace fuel, and ignite it first for the purpose of warming the chimney and initiating the upward flow of warm air.

3. Open a door or a window!

Drywall or Plaster?

This age-old argument is even waged now on radio, television and in newspaper advertising. Which shall it be? Lath and plaster, or drywall (also called sheetrock)? They both have advantages and disadvantages. Some parts of the country have only one of these trades active, but where they compete, here are some of the pros and cons for you to consider:

Plaster	*Drywall*
Advantages:	*Advantages:*
Lowest noise transmission	Cheaper to install
Harder finished surface	Quicker to install
Easier to repair	Cleaner to install
More solid, thicker, smoother	Fewer minor cracks
Disadvantages:	*Disadvantages:*
More vulnerable to cracking	A thinner, flimsier material
Takes longer to install	Patterns of connection more visible
Messier during construction	Textured, stippled finish is cheap looking
	Poor insulator of sound

Lath and plaster is 7/8 of an inch thick:

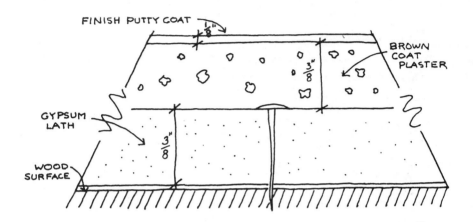

Drywall is available in these different applications:

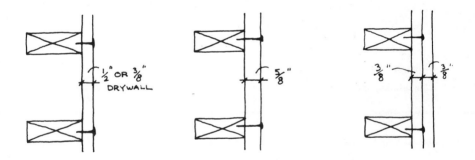

The 1/2-inch variety is the most common and is the one referred to in the pro-and-con list above. Drywall 5/8-inch thick is almost comparable to plaster, while the two sheets 3/8-inch thick liminated together is the best of all surfaces, since it has nearly the thickness of plaster, but the outside sheet can be glued instead of nailed to the first sheet, making a fine, strong, smooth surface with no nails and little putty showing. It is quite costly to apply.

In areas of the country where the plastering trade flourishes, it is best to give the nod to plaster houses because of the noise-transmission factor. In any event, you would do well to think twice about buying one with 1/2-inch or thinner drywall on the walls.

Decks—The Achilles Heel of the House

Decks, porches, or balconies with living spaces under them can be a constant source of grief if they are not 100 percent water-proof. Examine carefully these vulnerable areas from the rooms underneath them and try to determine if there is any evidence of previous water damage from signs of staining or discoloration. If you detect anything, question the seller unmercifully to find out what the problem has been and if satisfactory repairs have been made.

Particularly treacherous points in old decks are where posts penetrate the deck material, where the deck meets the wall of the house, and where any seams of covering material like canvas or fiber glass are overlapped.

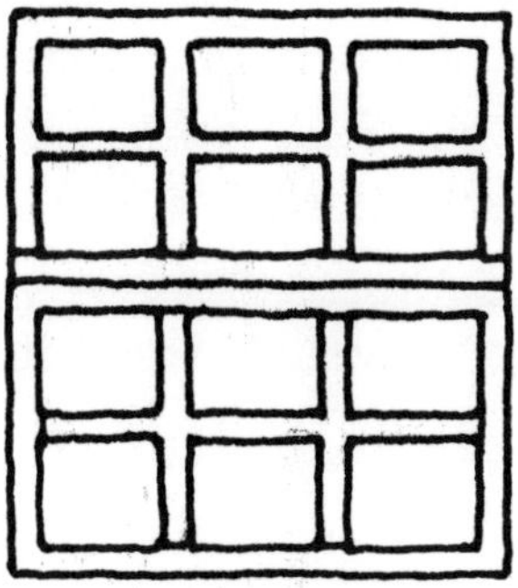

DOUBLE HUNG

CASEMENT

SLIDING

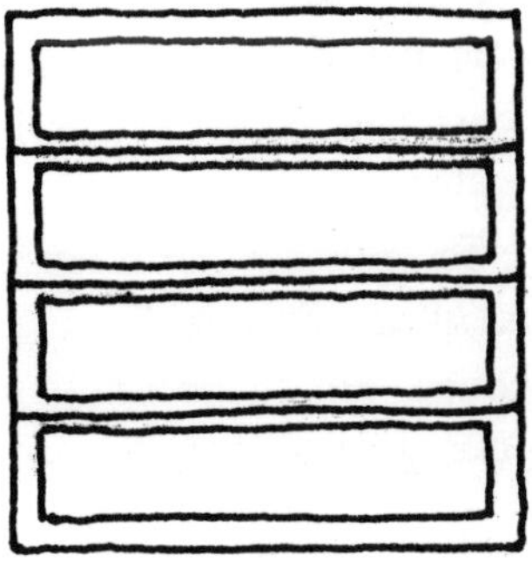

AWNING

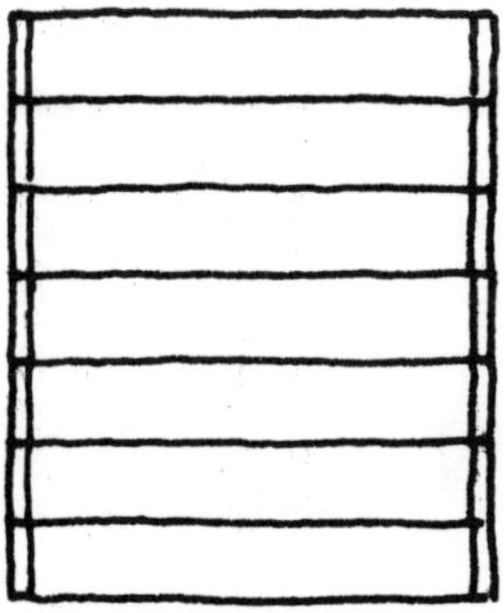

LOOVER

FIXED
OR
STATIONARY

Most decks (particularly canvas and magnesite) require some sort of service and maintenance to keep them waterproofed. So find out what method the seller has used and make a note of it.

Good slope, so water does not stand, is also important. This can be checked easily with a garden hose. You do not want leaky decks, so you should not allow yourself to be frustrated in finding out if they are dry.

Windows

Know the various types of windows. Most are seen in both wooden and aluminum designs, as shown in the drawings on the preceding page.

Old-fashioned double-hung and wood casement windows work out as the most dependable if they have been weatherstripped and well maintained. If they have been neglected, the cost of replacement is usually reasonable—that is only if the frames are good, however. In addition, aluminum sash can be ordered specially to fit the old wood frame at a cost just a little higher than the cost of stock aluminum sizes.

Windows with double-thick insulating (called "thermopane") glass are a tremendous asset to a house where temperatures or outside noise are factors to contend with. These windows are quite costly and deserve extra credit in totaling up a house's assets. Heating and air-conditioning costs can be reduced at least 20 percent when this double-thick glass is used. Additionally, they have the advantage of reducing sound from the outside. This latter can be quite a factor if you are locating near an airport, freeway or even a well-traveled road.

The lower corners of wood windows and their sills are excellent places to check for wood rot or termites. It is assumed you will have a termite report (more about this later) but that only occurs when you arrive at the escrow stage. This sort of preliminary check at least alerts you to a possible problem of larger scale.

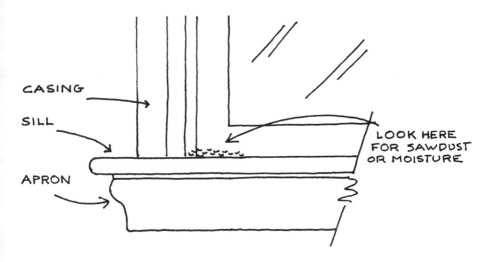

List of Subcontractors

If the house is not too old, the seller should still have a set of plans available. Also ask him for a list that includes the contractor and—more importantly—the subcontractors. These trades will doubtless not service the house free, but at least they are familiar with it and might know shortcuts to solving some of the problems that are sure to come up. They could help answer any critical question prior to going to escrow on the house that might affect your decision as to whether to make offer on it or not—or whether to include any contingencies concerning certain aspects of the structure that should have professional inspections.

Building Inspection—And How to Go About It

If an older house poses an intriguing blend of picturesqueness and attractive price, but you are shaky on many of the structural points covered so far, it is money and time well spent to hire a professional building inspector to go through the house for you and give you a report. Very often these men are retired building officials who really know their profession. Fees for this work usually run from $50 to $125. The city building department or perhaps the city license bureau should be able to furnish you with some names and telephone numbers of men practicing this service. Failing this, a nearby city's building department usually has some current inspectors who would moonlight the job for you in the evenings or on the weekend for a comparable fee.

Summary

1. Check setbacks, height limits and encroachments.

2. Be sure garage requirements have been met and are of adequate size. Also, be sure garage has not been altered.

3. Do not turn your nose up at elevated wood floors—they have some advantages over a slab.

4. Know the value of hardwood flooring: it is permanent, and wall-to-wall carpeting is not.

5. Look for house cracks that indicate foundation damage; then inspect the foundations for further evidence.

6. Inquire about vapor barriers around the outside edge of the house.

7. Look under the house; look in the attic.

8. Shun unorthodoxy in fireplace construction; visualize fireplace rooms completely and properly decorated. Be sure that the fireplace *mass* does not preclude this.

9. Covet plastered walls and laminated drywall; eschew 3/8- or 1/2-inch drywall.

10. Examine decks with a vengeance. Get solid answers from the seller on condition of decks. Inquire as to the method of maintenance.

11. Know what kind of windows the house has. Make notes. Old double-hung wood windows are usually the most watertight, so do not shun them for aluminum.

12. Prize highly any house with double-thick glass.

13. Obtain a list of the contractor and subcontractors, and the plans if they are available.

14. Engage a professional building inspector on older, more complicated homes.

17
THE OPERATION OF THE HOUSE— BASIC UTILITIES, KITCHEN AND SERVICE ROOMS

Utilities—Be Sure You Have Them All

These are the basic utilities that your house should have:

Sewer	Natural gas (some areas)
Water	Telephone
Electricity	Television cable (some areas)

These facilities come onto the property from sources *outside* of your lot. Make it your business to find out if all are available, the method of connection on any that do not serve the house, and the cost of installation on any you might desire that have not been brought up to the edge of your lot.

Sewer (including septic tank or cesspool) can usually be taken for granted; but, as previously stated, you should find out which kind of sewage disposal the house has. The city or county usually controls the sewer operation, but sometimes there is a private water or sewer district in which the connected homeowners own stock. Special provisions and restrictions go with such private companies, and you should track this information down if you would be served by one of them.

143

Water, which again can usually be taken for granted on previously subdivided lots, should be looked into from the standpoint of source (city, county, private water district, etc.), quality (soft, hard, etc.), and quantity (can you get all you want, or is the quantity restricted?).

Electricity is usually furnished by a regional power company of some sort with rates normally governed by a public utilities commission. Sometimes a builder will be intrigued into furnishing an "all-electric-house package." He will have all-electric kitchens, only electric dryer outlets, electric water heating and, perhaps, electric room heating and air-conditioning to the exclusion of any gas whatsoever. He is sometimes induced to do this by a bonus of twenty-five to one hundred dollars per house offered him by the local electric company, plus whatever saving he might make in not supplying any gas service at all to the houses.

Natural gas, where it is available, affords an inexpensive means of heating rooms, heating water, cooking and drying clothes. The exclusion of it entirely where it is otherwise available to the rest of a community deprives the buyer of appliance options he might otherwise have. It saddles him, in some cases, with higher utility costs, and it most assuredly detracts from the resale value of the house at a future date. Debate long and hard about buying a house without natural gas if it is available to those around you. Such a house is unnecessarily handicapped.

Telephone is usually provided either overhead or underground by the local telephone company. However, once in a while, you are on the borderline of two different companies. If this is the case, be sure you realize that local calls could be much more expensive if your center of calling interest lies across the border in enemy telephone territory. You will want to do the bulk of your local calling within your own system.

Television cable will become an increasingly important feature as services improve and paid television services develop. Even in areas of excellent reception, the cable companies are gradually beginning to make their contributions felt. First-run motion pictures and sports events are the obvious offerings, but the future will probably hold innovations in this potentially exciting field.

Trash pickup, while not strictly a utility, is certainly a vital service. Find out about trash collections, if there is a city or county charge for the service, and the days that collection takes place. There are sometimes requirements about segregating trash, the amount of yard clippings and the manner of packaging, permissible size of containers used, etc. The city engineering or public works department usually has printed guidelines for this.

Carmel, California, may not be the only city in the United States that does not have home *mail delivery* (because of not wishing to have house numbers), but you might assure yourself that you will be receiving normal mail delivery at the house of your choice.

The All-Important Kitchen

The kitchen operates as sort of a control tower in many homes. Therefore, the disposition of its appliances and cabinets is most important. There is an infinite variety of kitchen-cabinet arrangements possible, and most builders are aggressively aware of the sales appeal of this feature of the house. Therefore, a strong likelihood exists that these cabinets will be adequate in a house built for sale to the general public.

Rule of thumb calls for about twenty-five running feet of counter space in the kitchen, with the commensurate amount of upper cabinets over most of this area. This is a pretty good yardstick in evaluating an older home. This is not to say that an older home is lacking if it does not have built-in cabinets like most tract houses. Quite the contrary! Sometimes inadequate counter space can easily be made up for by the use of an old-fashioned kitchen table or butcher's table or block. Sometimes even kitchen-type furniture like a Welsh dresser, a dry sink, a French commode or a bureau could be used, as long as there is sufficient room in the kitchen. Similarly, the lack of cabinet space can easily be offset by a walk-in pantry closet with floor-to-ceiling shelving—quite an asset these days. Or perhaps an adjacent service porch has plentiful pantry or canned-goods shelf space available.

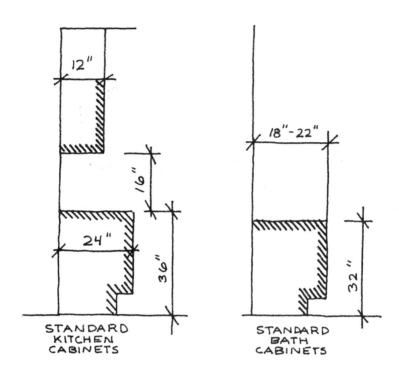

STANDARD KITCHEN CABINETS

STANDARD BATH CABINETS

In checking any doubtful sizes of cabinets, it is helpful to know that standard cabinet dimensions are as follows:

Kitchen counter height	36″
Bathroom pullman height	32″
Stand-up (or stool) bar height	42″
Table or desk height, or vanity	29″
Dishwasher width	24″
Refrigerator width	36″
Kitchen lower-cabinet depth	24″
Kitchen upper-cabinet depth	12″

Here is a chart of cabinet features explaining how they rank as to quality:

	POOR	ADEQUATE	BEST
Wood	softwood, pine, painted	cedar, birch, ash, mahogany	oak, teak, walnut, cherry
Doors	plain lip	flat panel	raised panel
Inside hardware	clip catch		magnetic catch
Drawer hardware	plastic guide	single roller	double roller
Drawer bottoms	Masonite	plastic	Marlite (smooth)
Drawer sides	3/8" ply		1/2" pine
Drawer back	1/2" pine	3/4" pine	3/4" pine
Door hinges	exposed	partially exposed	washington pin (concealed)
Splashes in kitchen	4"	8"	full height
Shelves	permanent		adjustable

Cabinet Counters

As to counters of tile, Formica or simulated marble, they are a matter of taste and decor, with little cost differential. Marble, stainless steel and laminated maple counters, on the other hand, represent premium selections costing almost twice as much and should be graded accordingly. Splashes behind kitchen cabinets should run full height to cabinets above. Splashes in baths are normally 6 to 8 inches, depending on the size of pullman and tile modules.

Washer and Dryer

These appliances are ideally located near bedrooms and bathrooms and not in some remote garage area. This was a nice feature of the clothes chutes in older, large, two-story homes. At least they provided one easy way for the clothes to get to the washing area, and if there was a dumbwaiter, they had an easy way to get back.

Occasionally, the washer and dryer are located on a second floor. Check to see if there is an overflow collection pan and a drain under the washer. They have a tendency to overflow their drains from time to time, and the resultant problem can be catastrophic.

Note if the dryer outlet is gas or electric or, hopefully, both. This will affect whether or not you can use a dryer you may already have.

ELECTRIC DRYER
RECEPTACLE
LOOKS LIKE THIS

Also, there should be a vent to the outside for the lint thrown off during operation of the dryer. If this is lacking, a trick is to place a nylon stocking over a short vertical projection of the dryer vent (just enough to get it out from behind the machine). From time to time it can be discarded full of lint and another stocking installed.

18
THE PLUMBING,
AND DOES IT WORK?

The Water Service—Where It Starts

The water service comes onto the property through a standard-sized supply line furnished by the city—most generally this is 1-1/2 inches in diameter. The homeowner purchases the meter on the new house, and it is subsequently passed on from one owner to the next. The 5/8-inch meter (now rare) is the smallest size, with 3/4 inches the most common, followed by 1 inch, then the commercial sizes of 1-1/2 inches and 2 inches. (The inches referred to is the size of the meter orifice.)

After the water emerges from the meter on the house side, the plumber usually serves the house with a pipe size the next fraction larger than the meter: a 1-inch pipe serving the house out of a 3/4-inch meter.

For a house having four or more bathrooms and a fairly good-sized yard, a 3/4-inch meter is usually too small; a 1-inch meter with a 1-1/4-inch supply line to the house would be the right size. While the 3/4-inch meter is probably adequate most hours of the day, at times of peak demand, such as when irrigation water is being used and clothes are in the washer, the pressure would likely be quite low within the house.

Test the adequacy of the water pressure and supply system by turning on the hose bibb nearest the main turnoff valve and then trying the pressure at the lav or sink inside. A decided weakness in the water pressure and supply system at these nearby sources merits a check of the meter size or the type of pressure the community as a whole is experiencing.

The Water Pipes

Examine the water piping in accessible areas like at the water heater, under the house or in the attic. It is the system of hot-and-cold-water piping that is a potential source of trouble in the plumbing systems of older houses. If the piping is galvanized iron, be forewarned that it just does not hold up in areas of hard or corrosive water. It tends to develop electrolysis. Look for a collection of saltlike deposits at the connections, or for a darkening rust color. Then shine a flashlight on wood surfaces that lie beneath water piping, and on the top of the water heater and at valve locations.

When these old, galvanized-iron water systems start to deteriorate, they usually give up all at once or in so many places that it necessitates the replacement of the entire water-piping system. Copper piping is much more dependable.

Investigate the water pressure within the house by turning on three or four fixtures at the same time, using different bathrooms. Any question about adequacy of pressure should cause you to have a professional plumbing inspection. This could mean a replacement of the entire water system. So, beware!

Is There a Water Softener?

Inquire about the quality of the water and if the house should have a water softener. These are not difficult to install, and this service is usually done by the company providing the soft-water tank at the time of first service. Then they make a monthly charge of a few dollars, which covers replacing the tank of rock salt periodically. The tank should be located where it can be serviced without disturbing the occupants of the house—preferably in an outside service yard accessible from a back gate. The tank should not be located in a garage where the automobiles block the installation. Normal practice is to connect the hot water to the softener, assuring that hose bibbs do not dispense soft water to plants.

Toilets, Other Fixtures—The Jewelry of Plumbing

Luxury in plumbing fixtures is not as desirable as function and consistency. Toilets manufactured in a one-piece casting are more costly, slightly quieter and more sleek in appearance than the separate-tank type. They do not, however, vary much in efficiency. As a matter of fact, the very low silhouette types may be a bit sluggish in swirling water around the bowl due to the low position of the tank reservoir.

Where shortcuts show up most shamefully in tract housing and subdivisions is in the use of "pressed-steel" tubs, lavatories and sinks, and fiber-glass tubs and showers. You will want fixtures of cast iron with porcelain enamel coating. At first glance it is difficult to tell the difference. A pressed-steel tub is the easiest for you to test, for it will yield slightly to the pressure of a thumb or fist applied to the bottom; the cast-iron one will not. Also, it is more likely to be scratched, which you can clearly see. The use of such a fixture in a house should be a signal that cheapness has been consciously sought and no doubt exists elsewhere.

Plumbing valves offer another potential area for skimping. The fad for single-lever handles has spawned a bevy of unsatisfactory, cheap, short-lived products. However, the separate hot and cold valves can be bought cheaply too, and it is best to confirm that all valves are brass. Fortunately, valves can be replaced at no great cost. So unless there is evidence of a total replacement problem, the appearance of a single leaky faucet should be viewed more as a warning sign for lack of maintenance rather than a cue that all valves are defective.

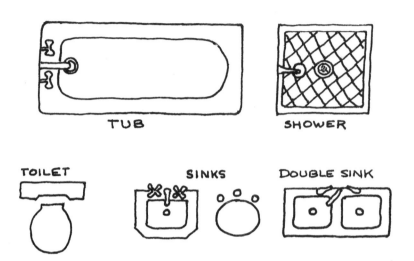

Check on the flushing of all toilets. The swirl of water should be quite active and evacuate the entire bowl. Refilling of the tank should be smooth and steady, not loud and hissing. Drainage of other fixtures should be checked as well. All should empty swiftly.

Water Heaters and Their Venting

This vital facility is expensive to replace—about $200 for a standard 50-gallon tank including the labor of installation. Ask, therefore, about its capacity and condition. The life of an average water heater is thought to be about ten years. However, it is not uncommon to have one rust out in three or four years, depending on the quality of the water and other factors like electrolysis at the input or output connection to the tank.

The majority of water heaters are manufactured in the 40- to 50-gallon sizes for homes and 30-gallon sizes for apartments. For larger sizes, such as 70 to 100 gallons, the cost increases dramatically. That is why most subdivision homes have maximum sizes of 50 gallons, which is inadequate for a family larger than four.

Prize highly a house with an oversized heater (greater than 50 gallons). Life will be a great deal more enjoyable. Remember, too, that you cannot always add a larger heater easily when the existing old one goes out. The larger sizes, while not much higher, are quite a bit thicker. Very often the builder has provided only a 2-foot-wide space, and the larger units need 2-1/2 feet, plus 6 inches or so of clearance.

There is one salvation. In replacing a water heater, find out about a "high-recovery" heater. In the 50-gallon size, for example, the standard B.T.U. input is about 42,000, whereas the high-recovery heaters are from 50,000 to 65,000 B.T.U.s. This makes quite a difference, and the cost is about $15 to $20 more.

Be wary of hot-water heaters (or gas dryers for the same reason) that sit on the floor of garages. These should be installed up off the floor by about 2 feet. This is so that when the pilot ignites the burners, it eliminates the risk of igniting any low-lying gasoline fumes from the automobiles.

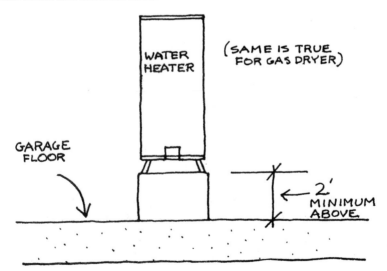

Notice if both high and low "combustion air" is provided to any water-heater enclosure. The low air is to feed the burners oxygen at the bottom of the tank. The high air relieves the heat and fumes that collect within the enclosure. Check that the heater tank itself is vented out through the room. Remember, that any gas heater needs these three vents:

1. Heat chamber or tank vent (through roof)
2. Low combustion air
3. High combustion air

Lastly, check to see, that water from the leaking of a water heater can drain safely to the garage or outside of the house. This is important! Or, failing this, see that a galvanized iron pan is installed underneath the heater to prevent its soaking the house floors irreparably. You can picture the damage that a deluge of 50 gallons of hot water could inflict!

What about Electric Water Heaters?

Electric water heaters are not as efficient, generally, as gas heaters. They do not recover as rapidly and they can be more expensive to operate. Their main advantages accrue to builders who have limited space and have trouble providing a vent.

Recirculating Water Systems

This special method of water piping is a definite plus. This is particularly valuable in a one-story, rambling house where you would otherwise have to wait an excessive length of time to get any hot water. Check this out if the bath you depend on is a great distance from the source of hot water. No one wants to wait the better part of a minute for hot water.

Interior Drainage Pipes—The Soil System

The "soil" or waste pipes that constitute the drainage system of a house are usually not the worst troublemakers. Underneath the house, a small leak is no great bother in the drainage system. Even in that vulnerable and potentially dangerous area between floors over a living area, a leak is generally a specific leak and not an indication that the whole drainage system is ready to expire (as can be the case in galvanized water piping).

One caution! Look for plenty of cleanouts. These are large plugs that, when removed, enable the plumber's snake or Roto-Rooter to unclog plugged drain lines. They are most valuable on outside walls, inasmuch as repairs can then be made without bringing the terribly messy reaming equipment inside the house.

A Word about Plastic Pipe

New houses are sometimes plumbed with *plastic pipe.* They are approved for drainage systems in many areas of the country. They can be destroyed by heat and can even catch fire, so their use is usually confined to single-family residences. Fundamentally, they provide a smooth interior surface, which aids in the movement of waste material through the lines. A major disadvantage (besides the fire problem) is the noise that water makes when it is running along the pipes. It can be a problem over first-floor living areas in two-story houses.

Find out if any of the drains are plastic. Do this by flushing an upstairs toilet (have the broker do this), and stand in the room below, listening. Water in a plastic drain makes a hollow, gurgling sound. You cannot mistake it. There is no easy solution, except to call a plumber and have him change the drain to cast iron. As for using plastic pipe for vents, soil pipe in the ground or even over utility and garage areas, there can be no objection.

Plastic water pipe is available, but its use is restricted to landscaping and sprinkler work outside the house. It, too, is vulnerable

to excessive heat and is therefore not satisfactory for interior use
in connection with the hot-water system.

The Gas Piping System

The gas system, like the water system, needs controlling valves
to turn it off not only at the main line entering the property and
house, but *at each fixture or appliance location.* Be sure to check
to see if these inlets can be separately controlled—not only for
maintenance and replacement, but for quick safety precautions in
case of leakage.

Check on the galvanized gas pipe as well. It can deterioriate
sometimes just due to moisture in the air and excessive age.
Specific leaks are checked out by applying soapy water and
waiting to see if it bubbles, much like testing for a tire leak.

19
ELECTRICITY—
THE HOUSE'S
NERVOUS SYSTEM

Electric Wiring

In checking on the adequacy and safety of the electrical wiring, it is helpful to know the various types used in construction over the years.

Knob and tube was the first and most primitive form of wiring. It resembles wires on a miniature old-fashioned power pole, with the positive and ground wires run separately and parallel as in this drawing:

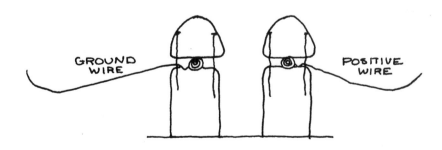

GLASS INSULATOR

GROUND WIRE

POSITIVE WIRE

In theory, this was a perfectly acceptable way of running wiring, except that as time wore on, the installation was subject to damage. Rats sometimes gnawed at the covering of the wires. General bumping and snagging of the wires occurred in crawl spaces and attics. The knob-and-tube wiring in a house is usually slated for replacement somewhere along the line.

Romex is wiring self-contained within a thick fabric or plastic shield. This is acceptable for most 110-volt residential wiring these days. It can be installed by drilling holes and pulling it through and stapling it without any housing of any kind. This speeds up the wiring process over the following types considerably.

Flex is the ribbed, metal tubing that looks like metal hose and bends in all directions. Flex is used for 220-volt wiring in most houses, and some communities require the entire house wiring to be in flex. Its full name is flexible conduit.

Rigid is the nickname given regular pipe or rigid conduit. It is the safest and most expensive method of installing wiring and is usually required for commercial, industrial and high-density residential use in apartment houses, triplexes and fourplexes. After this piping or tubing is in place, wiring is pulled through in the same manner as with flex.

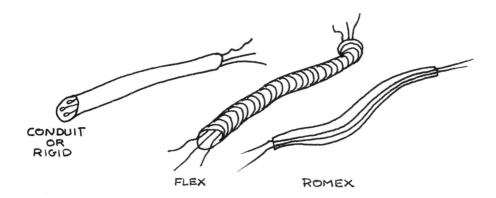

CONDUIT
OR
RIGID

FLEX   ROMEX

Following is a checklist of good features in electric wiring. Many of these are standard requirements in local city and county electrical codes.

Exterior Lighting—Important Checkpoints

—Is there adequate lighting around the house for evening enjoyment and security, plus convenient switching location such as at the entry hall, the living room, the family room? Ideally, some yard lighting should be switched from the master bedroom as an additional security measure.

—Is lighting provided around the garage and service yard, together with plug receptacles in the garage for tools, vacuum, extra freezer, battery charger, etc.?

—Are there waterproof receptacles provided in any patio areas for connecting barbecues, heaters, rotisseries, spotlights, etc.?

—Is there plenty of light at the front or back door or at any other place where anyone might enter or leave the house, plus convenient switching at that location?

—Is there lighting at the main electric service panel so you can see breakers and labeling without using a flashlight?

Interior of the House—Is It Satisfactorily Switched?

—Is there good "sequential" switching so that when proceeding through the house from one room to another, the switching enables you to leave a lighted room by any of its doorways and proceed on to another lighted room as you switch off the light in the room behind you? This checking calls for careful touring of the house. Note: When there are two switches controlling one (or more) lights, that arrangement is called a "3-way switch." Three switches controlling lights are called "4-way switches." This seemingly perverse nomenclature derives from the inclusion of the light or lights being controlled as one part of the switching group. Thus a house with good "sequential" lighting will have many 3-way and 4-way switching setups.

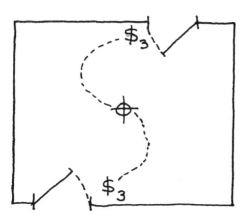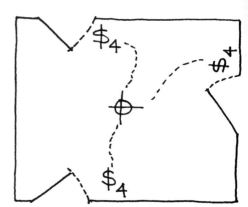

—Are there overhead fixtures or switched plugs in *every* room? Normally switched plugs are installed "half hot." This means that one plug in the double receptacle is not controlled by the switch and remains active or "hot" at all times.

—Are there duplex receptacles every 12 feet of wall space?

—Are there some floor receptacles where lamp cords cannot conveniently reach the walls of rooms?

—Are there four duplex receptacles in the kitchen?

—Is there 220-volt power provided for oven, cooktop, dryer, air-conditioning, pool heater?

—Are there duplex receptacles in all baths?

—Is there good bathroom lighting?

—Are there TV outlets in all rooms where there might be viewing?

—Are there telephone outlets prewired throughout the house to reduce any exposed telephone wires?

—Is there a built-in TV and FM antenna?

—Is there some type of intercom and proper door chimes?

—Is there flush, recessed lighting in various places throughout the house? This reflects the thoughtfulness and farsightedness of a good builder.

—Do closets and wardrobes have their own lighting?

—Are switches of the modern silent or semisilent type, or do they make a loud snapping noise when tripped?

The Main Electric Service or "Panel"

Electricity enters the property either by means of an overhead "drop" or, preferably, an underground service feed. Then comes the power company's meter box and a main switch location. The service, or panel, encompasses the individual circuits, ranging from 30-amperage breakers for the 220-volt oven, range and dryer, etc., to the 15-amperage breakers for common 110-volt circuits for various plugs, lights, etc.

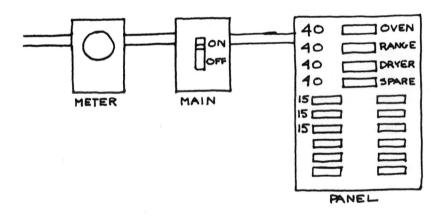

The capacity of the service panel determines how many circuits can be fed into the house. There is usually a place on the panel (often a small metal label) that specifies the total amperage. A small tract house, for example, can get along nicely with a 100-amp panel and still have extra unused places for circuits and room for additional electrical requirements. Look to see if there are empty circuit locations on the panel face. If not, you may be stuck with the cost of replacing the panel or adding a subpanel, both rather expensive changes. A 100-amp or 125-amp panel will not suffice for a medium-to-large home with extensive yard lighting, an electronic oven, air-conditioning, swimming-pool pump, range, oven, dryer, etc.

Here is a crude rule of thumb to show you the approximate size of electric service that should be used with certain areas of square footage:

2,000 square feet to 3,000 square feet: 100-amp panel
3,000 square feet to 4,000 square feet: 125-amp panel
4,000 square feet to 5,000 square feet: 150-amp panel

Remember, you are checking the service for its ability to accept *new* circuits above and beyond its present load. It would be a comforting feeling to know that the panel was sufficient for your projected needs and would not have to be replaced.

Telephone Service—Don't Be Gerrymandered!

Check on the availability and adequacy of this service. Learn if there is anything strange about your number listing or the company serving you. Do not think you are being served by the obvious large telephone company in the area only to find out that because of certain geographical boundaries you are being served by a small, struggling company that charges you long-distance rates just to call across the street because that happens to cross their boundaries. *This can happen!* So do not get trapped.

Television Cable Service

Most sellers will inform you of the status of cable television as it affects the property. If they do not, raise the question yourself. As indicated in our utilities checklist, the future holds a vast growth potential for this facility, and it could rival free television as a mainstay of the living rooms of America. Many builders and homeowners selling their houses have made provisions for easy and inexpensive hooking up with the system if it is not yet installed. Generally this consists of:

—Access to the underground or overhead source of eventual service.

—Providing a master 300-ohm TV cable from this access area to central location (attic, cabinet or closet within the house) where all TV leads from individual rooms are gathered.

—Providing a 110-volt AC outlet at that location for a signal amplifier.

With these provisions made, the connection to television cable facilities should be very inexpensive.

Electronic Security System—Your Own Safety Link

Increasingly, the consideration of security of the home is making its impact on today's home buyer. Several systems have been developed, including wiring a home alarm system to the local police department where they will accept such direct communication.

However, the most common arrangement calls for an electronic "bugging" of all ground-floor doors and some windows. These connect to a loud alarm of the ambulance type, which is set off if the bugged circuit of locked doors and windows is broken by an intruder.

Some condominium sales are stimulated by elaborate security systems extending to garage areas and entrance doors by means of closed-circuit television. At least be aware of these innovations and work them into your inquiries and plans if they seem appropriate where you are looking.

20
HEATING AND
AIR-CONDITIONING

This Is Your Source of Warmth

Heating systems, like water heaters, must not only be vented from the heater itself all the way up through the roof (if gas is involved), but they also need to have high and low combustion air vents for the heating closet for the same reasons as the water heater: the low air to provide oxygen for the burners, the high air for the relief of unburned gas fumes and heat captured within the room.

Give high marks to heating systems that distribute their warm air underneath the slab or wood floor. They are usually cheaper to operate because rooms tend to stay warmer with the ducting running underneath them. Also, heat emanating from low rather than high registers warms the rooms more efficiently by taking advantage of the fact that warm air rises.

Check to see that all rooms, including baths, have heating outlets. Another tract builder's shortcut is to leave heat out of the baths and kitchen. Make a separate tour of all of the rooms of the

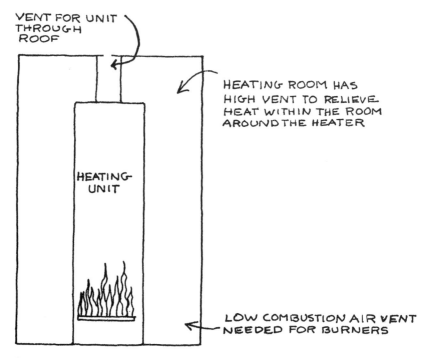

VENT FOR UNIT THROUGH ROOF

HEATING ROOM HAS HIGH VENT TO RELIEVE HEAT WITHIN THE ROOM AROUND THE HEATER

HEATING UNIT

LOW COMBUSTION AIR VENT NEEDED FOR BURNERS

house to ascertain the adequacy of the system. Of great importance to the efficiency and low operating cost of the system are the return-air grills normally located in central halls and living areas. These indicate some recirculation of previously warmed air within the house. The other type of system, which utilizes no "return air" or "used air," is called a "pressure system"; it derives all of its air from the outside. This type of system is cheaper to install but more expensive to operate and less efficient in heating. It is virtually impossible to convert a pressure system to air-conditioning without expensive remodeling.

Most homeowners know approximately what it costs to heat their homes as the result of comparing winter with summer utility bills. Ask about this expense, particularly if you sense an inadequate or antiquated system. Be aware, though, that the old hot water or gas- or oil-fired systems located in basements, which relied much on natural heat rise rather than pumps or fans, were often very good systems and relatively cheap to operate. Their big disadvantage was in the cost of installation because of their immense burners, tanks, ducts, plenums and damper blades, a cost which is of no concern to you as a buyer.

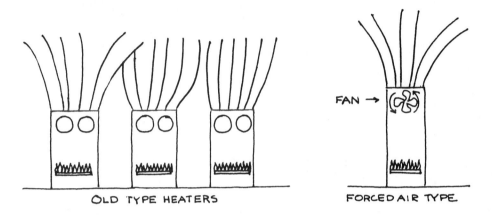

OLD TYPE HEATERS   FORCED AIR TYPE

Filters are a vital part of any forced-air type of heating and air-conditioning, where the rapid movement of air is involved. Be sure that these areas are accessible, since someone should change or clean the filters at least once a year in temperate climates and more often in cooler areas where equipment receives harder use.

A Warning about Horizontal Furnaces

The heat-exchanger chamber is where the air is warmed, and in the horizontal or "reclining" type of heating unit that chamber is subject to metal fatigue and corrosion, a condition which could cause a severe fire hazard. Have the seller call the gas company and get a clean bill of health on the horizontal heater if it is more than five years old, because trouble here could be of the worst kind.

If You Are Thinking of Adding Air-Conditioning . . .

There are several areas that have to be investigated if you intend to add air-conditioning to a home and you want to keep expenses within a certain budget:

—Existing ducts must be larger than the minimum sizes required for simply room heating.

—There must be a place for one or more condenser units *outside the house or in the garage.* They make a great deal of noise and vibration.

—The enclosure of the existing heating equipment needs to have an extra two or three feet above the unit to accommodate the refrigeration coil and air cleaner.

—Refrigeration lines (the size of a couple of garden hoses) have to be run from the condensers to the heating-equipment areas. They are hard to conceal and usually require some structural remodeling.

—Return air is a necessity. That is why an air-conditioning conversion is much easier if there is already a good return-air layout in the existing heating system.

—Extra power (usually 220 volts) is needed for the condensers.

Sometimes this conversion is made easy by the thoughtfulness of a farsighted builder, but more often than not you are on your own and will have to face some remodeling costs for this addition.

What about the Air-Conditioning Already Existing?

Air-conditioning is either gas or electric, the most common being the electric type. The principles involved are similar and are comprised of basic elements shown in the drawing:

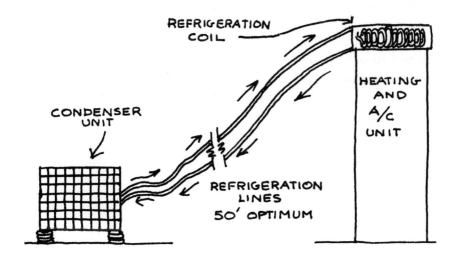

Rule of thumb for the tonnage required to cool a residence is as follows:

SQUARE FOOTAGE OF LIVING SPACE	TONS A/C REQUIRED
2,000	4 tons
3,000	6 tons
4,000	8 tons

Therefore, if the house you are looking at is in the 3,000-square-foot category, it should have about 6 tons of air-conditioning. "Ton" refers to the weight of the amount of air that the unit will move and cool in one hour.

After finding out the age of any existing equipment, the most vital information concerns the routing and the sizing of the ducts. Provided it is a well-known make and an original installation in the house, the equipment can be maintained and repaired in such a manner to keep it functioning in good condition for quite a few years. However, if the system has been added, the ductwork may be insufficient, the return-air arrangement inadequate, and it would then be very costly to alter the system because of the structural problems you would face.

A perfect return-air system would have air feeding back into the refrigeration coil and air-handling unit from all rooms into which the refrigerated air had been delivered. Obviously, this requires as much ducting for the return-air as for the originating cool-air ducts. This arrangement is typical of a commerical installation, where long use and large numbers of people demand a thoroughly engineered system. Usually in a residence, though, it is sufficient to return air only from the major rooms, eliminating baths, dressing rooms, halls, the service porch, etc., and in some cases, minor bedrooms. A good return-air system also helps keep costs down by recirculating cold air, just as it does with warm air.

Also, the *quietness* of a system needs to be considered. The more remote the condenser units are from the living area, the better the installation—up to a point. These units would ideally be located outside the house, preferably on a separate concrete slab. A location on the roof may still cause some vibration and should be checked out by turning on the equipment and listening. A garage installation for the condensers (called "through the wall" condensers), is fine, except that the garage is often too remote from the inside fans and the refrigeration lines lose efficiency beyond 60 or 70 feet. Therefore, this condenser separation is a form of compromise.

Also check the sound level of the fan units inside the house to see that they are well insulated from rooms you will be using for day-to-day living.

Warranties—Are There Any Left?

Ask about any warranties that might not have expired. This applies to all mechanical equipment. You might be surprised to find that some are still in effect.

Insulation—The Temperature Type

Insulation is valuable in any home, both to keep heat in and to keep cold out. It helps stop transmission of some sound through walls and ceilings, but not as efficiently as it stops heat from passing.

Insulation generally takes these forms:

Wall insulation between studs.

Specific insulation or wrapping around plumbing pipes and machines.

Ceiling insulation in the attic.

Crawl-space insulation under ground-floor wood floor.

Roof insulation under the tar-paper membrane.

The ceiling and roof insulation are the most critical with respect to air-conditioning, because the large, horizontal roof plane is quite vulnerable to the warming sun. The combination of an insulated roof membrane, a well-ventilated attic and rock wool blown in on top of the underlying ceiling joists makes the best residential heat shield you can imagine.

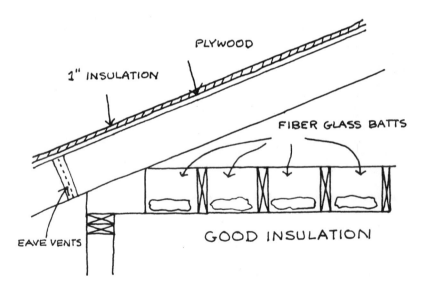

Be very critical of a house where insulation has not accompanied the installation of the air-conditioning. In adding air-conditioning, it is understandable why insulation has not been put into the walls: This would mean tearing apart all of the outside walls of the house to get it in. However, an attic space is quite accessible, and insulation can easily be blown in on top of the ceiling joists. This feature can cut air-conditioning costs and lighten the load on the equipment from 30 to 40 percent.

There is an easy way to tell whether the walls have been insulated. Look for any cover plates for television or telephone outlets in the *outside walls.* Remove one of them with a knife or small screwdriver and search around inside with your finger. Unlike electric receptacles, there is usually no metal can or box behind these outlets, and you will be able to feel and see if any insulation is inside the wall.

Inspect the attic through the access hole to see if there is insulation material on top of the ceiling joists. As for insulation under the tar roof membrane, it is doubtful if that would have been added with the air-conditioning, although if the system was put in when the house was new, the insulation might have been part of the original specifications. Such roof insulation is particularly critical over rooms with open-beam ceilings and no attic.

Insulation—The Sound Type

Insulating material nailed to each side of a common wall or placed in that wall is virtually ineffective as a sound-deadening agent. The most effective means is to *double the walls and ceilings structurally* so that insulating board can be applied to separate rather than identical, shared wood members. This is the way condominium units should be separated, and you should go to some pains to check the methods of insulation that have been used. Remember there are two principle types of insulation involved here—one for temperature, one for sound.

21
REMODELING
FOR APPRECIATION
AND USE

Remodeling—Is It Ever Justified?

There is an oft-repeated adage to the effect that you get your money out of decorating but seldom out of remodeling. This is because almost every penny used in redecorating results in a visible change. It shows. Since decorating is more or less cosmetic, it affords an opportunity to apply a new and—hopefully—more attractive "skin" or facade to the surfaces treated.

Remodeling, however, assuming it concerns more than merely widening a doorway or making a pass-through, usually entails an alteration of the structure, frequently calling for new foundation footings, the moving of walls, reroofing, rerouting plumbing, heating, wiring, etc. Clearly, much of this expense will go for hidden, nondramatic structural changes. Unless a vast amount of new square footage is created, or unless room shapes and relationships are drastically improved, it is generally difficult to show how the high costs of remodeling will pay off from a strict investment point of view.

Of course, every situation is unique, and it would still be wise to explore remodeling opportunities, costs and potentialities where remodeling is not only easy to accomplish but is *certain* to enhance the value of the property. That is the light in which remodeling is touched on here. How can it bolster and further enhance your real estate investment?

As mentioned previously, the easiest and cheapest remodeling is a scheme that extends the first-floor plan on the ground-floor level. This is simply "adding on." It can usually be achieved by spending little more than the current per-square-foot cost of new house production. That is, provided that the addition is not over-rich in plumbing, electrical and heating requirements. The high concentration of these mechanical elements would drive up the unit square-foot cost of remodeling as opposed to simply adding a bedroom, closets, a plain family room, rumpus room, or storage areas and garages.

The remodeling that is most costly involves partial demolition and second-story additions plus first-story alterations under bearing walls. A very crude rule of thumb is to estimate *double* the current per-square-foot cost for building a new house for the entire footage of the proposed remodel, including other areas affected.

An Example of Estimating Remodeling Costs

Let us say that 600 square feet needed to be added to the home's second floor and that 200 square feet on the first floor were affected because a new stairway had to be added, plus a coat closet, additional structural headers to carry the loads, and all the wall surfacing and floor covering. This brings the total area involved up to 800 square feet. While 800 square feet might cost around $16,000 to $20,000 simply to add onto the first floor, it could cost between $32,000 to $40,000 to add onto the second.

Basic Considerations in Remodeling

A. Structural
  1. Foundation
  2. Wood frame, including windows and doors
  3. Roofing

B. Mechanical
  1. Plumbing
  2. Electrical
  3. Heating

C. Finishing
  1. Cabinets, windows and door trim
  2. Plaster or drywall

D. Painting

Without breaking down all of the specialty trades involved with weatherstripping, tile, built-in appliances, etc., this easy eight-point list gives you the main elements of cost in evaluating the project. The basic subcontractor list that could be involved is quite lengthy.

As we go ahead with an analysis of what it will probably cost you to remodel, remember that this is all within the framework of looking at a house to *buy* and the hazards of counting on making it work through remodeling it. Somebody who is *already* occupying a house, already settled in a community, would have an entirely different view of a remodeling project than someone newly committing to relocating in a different house that *must* be remodeled to be made plausible. For the individual already satisfied with the general locale, the neighborhood and the basic house, remodeling can be an excellent means of revising the home to meet changed or enlarged needs without the expense and inconvenience of selling out and relocating.

This list of subcontracting trades and other elements is for rough estimating, or at least for furnishing you with an idea of the many personalities that could be involved in such a project.

Architect or designer

Engineer

Surveyor

Demolition

Building permit

Water meter (larger)

Utilities

Excavating

Grading, filling

Concrete foundations

Concrete slab

Concrete walks

Chimney, fireplaces

Masonry walls

Masonry walks

Rough lumber

Finish lumber

Rough carpentry

Finish carpentry

Plumbing

Temporary toilet

Structural steel

Sheet metal

Ornamental iron

Roofing

Decking

Lath and plaster

Drywall (sheetrock)

Fences

Insurance

Rough hardware

Finish hardware

Electric wiring

Electric fixtures

Intercom

Heating

Air-conditioning

Door and window frames

Doors

Screens

Cabinets

Stair work

Garage door and equipment

Glass

Sash, sliding doors

Mirrors

Shower and tub enclosures

Weatherstripping

Tile, Formica work

Marble work, mantels

Painting

Wallpapering

Vinyl floors, masonry floors

Carpeting

Built-in appliances

Insulation

Cleaning, removing debris

Landscaping

Sprinklers, drainage

Gates

Unit Costs

These are some "rule-of-thumb" unit costs that may prove helpful in figuring on remodeling work on a house that you are considering buying.

Air-conditioning with central refrigeration unit (2,000-square-foot home requiring about 5 tons)	$2,000-$3,000
Barbeque and vent, including electricity or gas	$500
Cabinets based on upper *or* lower base cabinets	$20 per running foot
Counter tops in either plastic or tile	$7 per running foot
Fencing in redwood or grapestake, 6 feet high	$2.50 per running foot
Flooring of tile	$2.50 per square foot
Hardwood oak flooring, sanding and refinishing	$2.50 per square yard
Fireplace and chimney, one story	$900
Fireplace and chimney, two story	$1,600
Insulating ceilings where attic is accessible	0.25 per square foot
Mirrors—installed	$3.00 per square foot
Paneling, utilizing prefinish plywood, installed	$1.25 per square foot
Plumbing fixtures installed	$400 to $500 per fixture
Roofing with shingles	$50 per hundred square feet
Wallpapering using 30-square-foot rolls	$6 per roll

The "Man Day"

Remember this very helpful hint in estimating workmen's costs in remodeling. Because of the time consumed in loading a truck with supplies, obtaining the supplies in the first place, driving to and from the project, setting up and later cleaning up tools and supplies, the amount of "man days" often determines the laboring costs of a job. Hiring the man himself, equipped with tools and a truck, and scheduling him into the field usually costs a subcontractor about $100 including various tax, fringe benefits, union contributions, etc. So if a wall looks like it might take one half a day to tear out, and a window opening an hour or so more to create, the subcontractor will figure that he will lose his carpenter for a day, and so the carpentry work should run around $100 for the total of the two jobs even though they really can be done in less time.

The Labor-Material Relationship

Although admittedly a crude guide for remodeling, in *new house* construction, the cost of labor and materials roughly equal one another in many areas of expense.

—Lumber costs approximately as much as the rough carpentry costs.

—Concrete for foundations costs much the same as the labor of digging footings, forming and supervising the pouring.

—Concrete costs for a slab relate somewhat to costs of grading, leveling, setting forms and screeds and finishing.

—Tile costs about the same as preparing beds and setting it.

—Heating ducts and equipment cost about as much as the labor to install them.

—Cabinets, masonry—all areas are miraculously comparable in materials and labor.

Because remodeling entails tearing out as well as constructing anew, the labor factor generally exceeds the cost of materials by a wide margin. If $1,000 worth of materials is required for a job, the labor would likely be double that, or $2,000. This one to two relationship would provide a rough estimating basis for quick figuring of remodeling.

The Time Necessary to Remodel

One important factor not to be overlooked in evaluating the disadvantages of remodeling is the inordinate length of time consumed by the project. In an extensive remodeling, when most of the "new-house" subcontracting trades are employed, it is not uncommon to have the time run to four or five months—almost the time needed to build a completely new house.

One unhappy idiosyncrasy of alteration work is that workmen are customarily harder to attract to a remodeling job than to new work for the simple reason that they cannot accurately predict the conditions they will have to deal with. It is harder for them to organize their scheduling patterns on remodeling as opposed to new work, where the commitment for entire days is certain and working conditions are far more congenial.

The most successful remodeling projects seem to be run by earnest, small contractors who work close to the job themselves and possess a high degree of organization ability, skill and versatility in several areas: carpentry, sheet metal, concrete, glazing, minor electrical work, plumbing and Formica installation, all of which lets them move the work ahead without having to call specialty trades and subcontractors to the job at every turn.

The Importance of Plans

If you are dead earnest about a new home that demands remodeling, have a designer or an architect prepare a sketch of the required work as quickly as possible. Either you or your broker should then obtain two or three estimates for the work before going further.

If regular working drawings are needed later on, they can be prepared under less rushed conditions, while the escrow time is elapsing. But the sketch or preliminary drawing will suffice for obtaining estimates. Naturally, for accomplishing simple changes or window or door openings, no drawing is really needed, and usually your broker can assist in getting a figure from a reliable subcontractor who will handle the whole thing for you.

Summary and Points of Emphasis about Remodeling

1. Enlarge first-floor areas—the cheapest to do.
2. Concentrate on increasing square footage, not just changing around what is there.
3. Emphasize what shows, minimizing the unseen and the structural.
4. Improve fluidity, vistas, traffic, enlarging rooms and spaces.
5. Minimize plumbing, heating, electrical, gas and masonry contributions.
6. Examine the subcontractor list and speculate on how *few* subtrades can accomplish what you have in mind.
7. Use proposed affected square footage to estimate remodeling costs.
8. Use unit costs to estimate specific remodeling costs.
9. Use man days and labor-material relationships to estimate.
10. Do not underestimate the time required to remodel extensively.
11. Get proper plans to estimate remodeling costs.

THE POTENTIAL OF DECORATING 22

Redecorating—The Best Way to Go

Remember our expression used very early in the book—"Look around you." This chapter is dedicated to sharpening your eyesight to the decorative potential of the houses you are shown. Some houses will lend themselves to easy decorating, while others all but preclude it because of such a strong thematic commitment ("heavy Spanish," "all glass," etc.). You must learn to sense the difference.

Consult a decorator if there is a house you are serious about and you want an expert estimate on what the redecoration will cost. Fees for decorative services vary greatly, but the one found acceptable by most knowledgeable clients is a flat fee plus a small percentage markup on the decorator's cost of materials and labor.

Carpeting and Floor Covering—Probably the Biggest Budget Item

Carpeting is not a material like hardwood or masonry—it is not intended for lifetime use. Therefore, unless you are buying a new house, the carpet may be scheduled for replacement in the near future. In making the budget decision on this, raise your sights above the multitude of bargain products available. It is much harder to clean cheap carpeting and to keep it clean. It will not last much longer than four or five years. Buy for quality and long life. Eschew faddish design and colors. Stick with enduring concepts, for new floor covering goes a long way toward improving a home.

If the house has handsome hardwood floors underneath the carpeting, but you want the continuity of wall-to-wall carpeting, consider leaving a one- to two-foot border around uniform, colored carpeting. The effect as shown in this drawing is striking, and you can enjoy the best of two ideas.

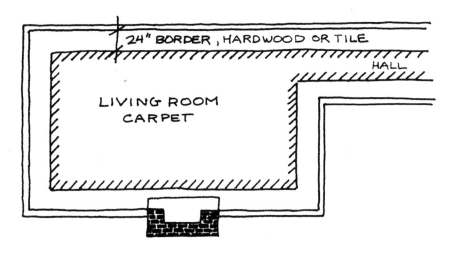

If the house has oak hardwood floors, you might consider using them as a more major decorative feature and only spotting around small area rugs. However, old yellow oak floors that look like gymnasium flooring are decoratively passé and should definitely be slated for sanding, staining and reworking. While hardwood floors generally cost the builder less than wall-to-wall carpet, if the carpet is due for replacement, do consider the rehabilitation of these floors. They need to be sanded down (professionally) and possibly grooved and doweled to resemble plank flooring. Then the floors should be stained dark, wax applied, and buffed. You have, as a result, a magnificent platform on which to build your decorative scheme. Flooring refinished in this manner costs about twenty to twenty-five cents a square foot.

If there are tile or masonry floors, try to capitalize on this feature. If the color is bad or they are dry and dead looking, keep in mind that they, too, can be stained to a deep uniform color, and waxed and buffed in order to achieve a decorative, attractive patina. Some brick can even be sanded prior to waxing to give it a smooth, worn look of aged brick. Tile or masonry floors are expensive for the builder to install, running upwards of twenty dollars a yard, so think twice before you take them out or cover them up with carpet. You may be spoiling a good thing.

Antiquated linoleum or vinyl flooring can be truly depressing. There have been so many advances in the field of plastic flooring materials that your choices are limitless. Visualize rooms like the kitchen, breakfast room, or service porch in the new brick designs, or vinyl patterns separated with colorful feature strips of contrasting material. Also consider for these rooms the new "outdoor carpeting" to lay over outmoded vinyl in the areas where liquids are a hazard.

Wall Covering—The Possibilities

Many things can be used to cover walls in your new house:

Wallpaper	Molding designs
Paneling	Mirrors
Fabric	Masonry
Full-length shutters, treillage	Draperies

The least expensive of these is wallpaper, and it is the one most likely doomed to failure in the hands of an amateur. The subtler papers are the most durable over the years, but when selecting designs it is often tempting to strike out for novelty. Deny this urge! Keep papers harmonious with draperies, upholstery fabric and carpeting, and vice versa. Spend time studying the color blend or "mix" of samples of these elements placed close together or mounted on a board.

Pay attention to the baths and small dressing rooms. They are good wallpapering candidates because they are too small for attractive furniture, drapes or much else in the way of decorative aid, except, perhaps, for mirrors. Old paper can be steamed off by the painter or paperhanger.

In addition to papering whole walls, be mindful that walls can also be done by applying borders, dados and molding effects combined with paper.

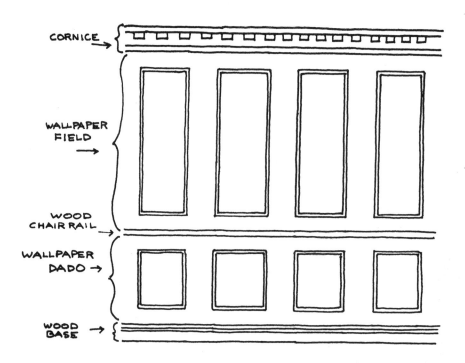

Moldings (the Frame around the Picture), and Doors

This brings us to the most underrated of decorative tools. Perhaps because of the enthusiasm for modern, clean-line architecture among most architects, or perhaps because of the builder's less lofty desire to cut costs of construction, the use of intricate moldings has diminished almost to the point of nonexistence in mass housing.

There is a type of modern house in which moldings are extraneous. This is the no-nonsense, hard-edged style, with high ceilings, crisp medical-clinic cabinets, doors and drawers of plastic, acres of glass and black oak on vinyl floors—the perfect setting for Italian steel furniture. The house for which you are shopping is not apt to be in this modish style; it is apt to be much more homespun and ordinary. In which case, do consider the addition of ample moldings. These are stock items at any lumber yard. The sketch contains some standard designs that would enhance any room of the house.

Bed mold at ceiling particularly desirable for main rooms of a house and where room is to be wallpapered. If ceilings are acoustic, this can still be done, but it simply does not fit as tightly to ceiling.

Crown mold can also be used.

Chair rail—pleasant effect in
halls, family room, dining
areas, also where dado effect
is desired; wallpaper above,
moldings in square or paneling
below.

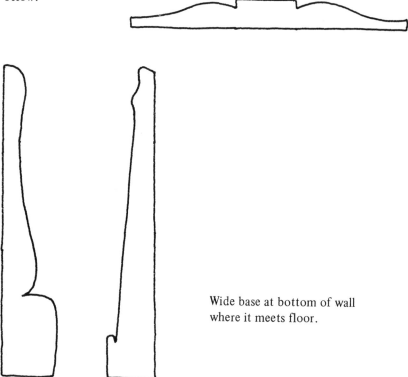

Wide base at bottom of wall
where it meets floor.

Wide door casing attractive in
principal room.

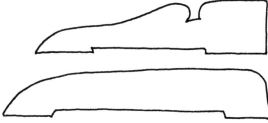

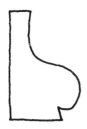

Panel mold very versatile in
making rectangles on walls,
embellishing plain stair skirts,
square below chair rail.

Stark "slab" doors can be enhanced by the following types of
designs using an applied "flat astragal" molding.

Flat astragal most useful in
"panelizing" rectangles for
wallpaper, creating design on
slab doors, etc.

Window Coverings

Draperies   Shutters
Valances   Curtains
Shades

Various combinations and designs of these elements offer a
boundless source of window coverings.

Sometimes the draperies can cover a whole wall effectively to
complete the luxurious and textural effect.

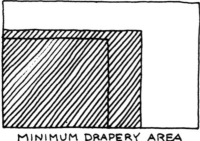

MINIMUM DRAPERY AREA

DRAPING THE WALL

Draperies are often the subject of discussion in buying a house
because they are detachable and can, therefore, legally be retained
by the seller. Decide first of all whether or not you really want his
drapes. Chances are he is anxious to leave them behind but wants
to attach some value to them. Actually, used drapes have hardly
any value at all, and there is no sense in allowing them to become
a negotiating factor if they will not suit your decorative objectives.
If in doubt, forget the old drapes.

Painting—Another of the Essentials

Painting is all important in the refurbishing of an older home,
but be alert to the variety of things that can be done with paint. In

addition to rolling on flat wall paint and enameling the cabinets and doors, this tradesman is often able to glaze (antique effects), grain (wood-grain effects) and may even do striping and mural work, useful in creating border effects on or around casings, cornices, mirrors, etc.

However, straight painting will be his greatest contribution, and depending on the amount of preparatory work involved, a rule thumb for painting one coat on the walls and woodwork for rooms of various size is:

LARGE	MEDIUM	SMALL
$1,000	$600	$300

Two coats on both walls and wood:

$1,500	$1,000	$500

This will help you roughly figure the cost of repainting.

Mirrors

These can be utilized decoratively for much more than merely looking at yourself. Whole walls can be covered with mirrors, an effect that is particularly useful in cramped entry ways, stair halls, narrow halls with jogs in them or abrupt endings, dressing rooms and baths and small bar areas. Antique mirrors with variations of silver and gold striations are useful where decor is semiformal. Mirrors can also be framed with moldings to decorate an entire dining room with a feeling of sumptuous elegance.

Hardware

Decorative hardware is fairly inexpensive to replace on major cabinets and doors that may cry for more attractive hardware.

Underscaled, oxidized door pulls cheapen and sadden the effect of this casework.

Door locks are rather expensive to replace throughout. Here again you might look at the house with an eye to improving the door latches in the major areas of the house or adding decorative escutcheons to some of the doors, which would simply be large surrounding metal pieces that would fit over the existing locks.

Chimney Pieces, Fireplace, etc.

These central and important elements must be made to look right or no decorating efforts will pay off. Massive outcroppings of lava rock or other eccentric owner or builder whims may leave you with a severe decorating obstacle that is very costly to remove. Wood paneling, mirrors, and plaster are all good covering materials, so you may be able to scale down one of these monstrous incinerators if the house you want is so cursed.

Stock chimney pieces can be bought of marble or wood. It is also possible to build up a marble or tile fireplace surround, and not very expensive. A simple surround, including inside returns and hearth, costs about $130 installed; this price would be typical for a medium-priced marble or travertine surround.

Tile surrounds are a little cheaper, and considering the vast quantity of domestic and imported designs available, these pose a ready solution in any home where they would blend with the decorative theme.

Stairs Can Be a Dramatic "Core" to the House

If the railing and balusters are skimpy, consider replacing them with good, decorative stair parts. If the iron is too plain, consider one of the numerous wrought iron applied castings called "plant-ons." Both upper and lower stairs and stair halls, as we discussed in an earlier chapter, must be inviting. This means plenty of natural and artificial light, and no closed-in feeling.

Some of this can be attained with decorating effects. Mirrors open up, lighten, heighten and widen. Improved light fixtures obviously help. Sunny, bright paper will help a confined stair.

Added Semistructural Elements

At very little expense, a form of light structural composition may improve a room or connecting room.

Screens	Divider
Grills	Arches
Shutters (large, full length)	Trellises

These addenda can often lend a completely new quality to the surroundings by improving a window opening or the aspect of a too square room, or creating a new room by separating a living room from a dining room.

PLASTER ARCHES

Electric Fixtures—An Easy Area of Improvement

This obvious category offers not only an opportunity for improving the functioning of the house through better lighting, but for improving the decor through more attractive and suitable fixtures. Old, unattractive sconces and underscaled chandeliers or ceiling fixtures are the most common offenders.

In areas of utility, such as the service porch, kitchen and baths, extra-high ceilings can be dropped down very effectively and economically by the installation of a luminous ceiling, provided there is some soffiting and cabinets do not reach full height (see sketch).

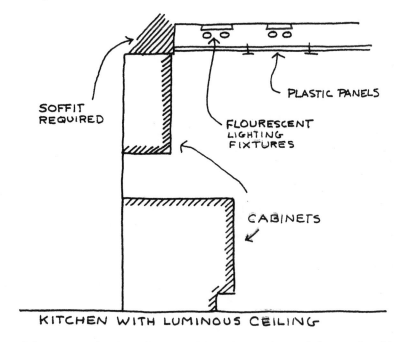

KITCHEN WITH LUMINOUS CEILING

Of course, this is only scratching the surface of decorating ideas and possibilities. The thought here is to point out the way toward a secure and fruitful home investment. Realizing how many opportunities are at hand, try to seek out houses where these decorative efforts would be the most productive—where your decorative schemes are not blunted by bad interior arrangement or too-major commitments to all-inclusive themes by the builder or previous owners.

23
PRICE AND NEGOTIATION– THE MAKING OF A DEAL

Is It a Buyer's or a Seller's Market?

Try to ascertain the character of the particular market in which you are shopping. Its reputation as a buyer's or as a seller's market is one of the criteria that can determine how far off the price you might legitimately make your first offer.

If there are numerous houses for sale and few buyers, you are in a buyer's market. Conditions are ripe for you to make a low offer. Under these conditions, an offer of 20 to 25 percent below the listed price is a good place to start. It will not win you any friendship with the seller, but in a sluggish market, why not try it? If there is little for sale and demand is great, you will have to offer closer to the listed price. Under these conditions, an offer of 10 to 15 percent below the asking price is perfectly respectable.

When the market is somewhere in between, either with many listings but good demand, or few listings and less demand, 15 percent off the listed price is a good middle-ground offering figure and should be taken seriously by your seller.

How Long Has the House Been on the Market?

Inquire as to the *listing history* of the house. To develop a complete picture, try to determine the background of the offering even prior to the present listing. It may have been on the market for more than a year, in which case your behavior as to offering can be a little different than if it were just recently listed.

Was the house built or bought by the present owner? When?

Has it ever been offered for sale before? When?

What was the offering price?

Have there been any previous offers?

Has the price ever been changed?

How long has the house been on the market currently?

A home that has just had its price reduced must have a length of time for the new lower price to "season." However, a home that has been offered for six months with no recent price reduction is certainly vulnerable to a low initial offer. A period of ninety days is considered sufficient for a good average exposure. If a property has failed to sell or attract offers in that length of time, the moment might have arrived for you to make a low offer.

OFFERING RANGE –	BUYER'S MARKET					
ASKING PRICE	39,000	40,000	50,000	69,000	79,000	89,000
FIRST LOW OFFER	25,000	32,500	40,000	50,000	58,000	65,000
OFFERING RANGE –	SELLER'S MARKET					
ASKING PRICE	30,000	40,000	50,000	60,000	70,000	80,000
FIRST LOW OFFER	27,000	36,000	45,000	54,000	63,000	72,000

What Is the Personality of the Seller?

Alongside the knowledge of the listing history of the house, place whatever you can learn about the personality of the seller:

Number, and ages of members of his family?

Reasons for selling?

Degrees of possible urgency?

From these and other facts you should be able to assay the type of reception any lower-than-normal first offer might receive.

Note: There is one peculiarity attending the first low offer on an overpriced house. A seller with a grossly overpriced property, while shocked at the disparity between the asking price and your low offer, has to face one awful truth. If his house had been fairly priced, your offer would have had a decent percentage relationship to it:

For example, say the following numbers applied: "Overpriced" listed house (the house should be listed at $80,000): $90,000. Offer: $65,000.

While this offer is 30 percent off of the listed price, it is only 20 percent off of the "fair," or more realistic, price.

If there had been such an offer, the seller would no doubt have turned it down. However, following that, he might well have indulged in some soul-searching as to the fairness of his initial price and may even have considered lowering it. In short, do not be daunted by the broker telling you that the seller has already turned down a low offer in the range you are considering. Who knows? There might have been special unacceptable terms included in the offer that the broker doesn't even know about. The simple knowledge of a turndown is not sufficiently informative to discount submitting the same low offer at a later date.

What in effect often happens is that the first low offer has softened up the seller and actually set the stage for another low offer quite similar to the first. The second stands a somewhat better chance of being accepted. Such is the phenomenon of an initial low, low offer. Many people may look at a house, but few put up a cash deposit and make a written offer. In addition to his afterthoughts about price, the seller always remembers the first low offer—perhaps with sort of a love-hate nostalgia—even though he turned it down. Therefore, learn the history of the listing and the background of any previous offers. This knowledge may work in your favor.

What about the Extra, Extraneous Items?

Even though you are keeping the price as low as possible in your initial offer, blast your seller with all of the other things you want at the time of the first offering. Do not wait to bring up such distractions at a later stage; this can be very upsetting to negotiations and provide a psychological excuse for the seller to break off the scenario of counteroffers. Do all of the nasty work at one time.

Typical inclusions that must be set forth in an initial offer are:

Lengthy escrow	All contingencies
Inclusion of carpets, drapes	Movable potted plants, shrubs, trees
Any freestanding appliances	Built-in-type furniture that can be
All first and second note pro-	moved
visions	Termite and pest agreement

Financial Terms

If an existing loan is to be increased or a new loan obtained, your offer will need to contain a *contingency,* allowing ten days to three weeks for the necessary investigation and removal of the contingency in writing. Often a way of making the hand fit the glove in this matter is to propose a *second trust deed* and note to be carried by the seller to make up any gap between the desired increase of institutional financing and the present loan. The next chapter is devoted to the finding and evaluating of the first trust deed commitment, but some words are now in order about proposing the carrying of a second trust deed in the offer.

A very valuable feature of the second trust deed is the ability to transfer it if you should sell the property. Therefore, there should be no *alienation clause* whereby it would be due and payable upon sale or transfer. This provision should be in your original offer.

Consider the man who works for a company that is always transferring him around the country. He certainly would not want to be paying off second-trust-deed balances whenever he had to sell a house, and there is no reason why you should be treated any differently by your seller. After all, if the house selling price is fair and you put up a down payment of $5,000 to $10,000, the seller's equity represented by the cash in hand and the second trust deed he would hold should be adequate for his protection no matter who owns the house.

Interest only? In order to keep your payments within reason for those initial months in the newly acquired house when costs multiply, ask for "interest only" payments for the first year, with principal payments to pick up at that time.

Also ask for as long-term a second as you can get—5 to 7 years, if possible. It is just that much more of a resale tool when you go to put the house on the resale market yourself.

The interest rate of the second trust deed can often be linked to that of the first. If it appears that the first might be anywhere from 7 to 8-1/2 percent, do not offer 8 or 8-1/2 percent on the second trust deed. Rather, say, "Second trust deed and note to bear interest to seller at the same rate as that approved by buyer for the first trust deed." This is fair and will not stick you with a higher rate on the second if you should manage to get a low-interest first trust deed.

Naturally, there should be no prepayment penalty for paying off the second, nor that nefarious wording, "Note may be paid off without penalty at the option of the seller (or with the seller's approval)." This nonsense is sometimes written down gratuitously by naive and dim-witted real estate brokers trying to phrase things legalistically. If granting such permission to the seller to let you pay off your own note is a specific demand of his, then it becomes a serious negotiating point, but for a broker to throw in this wording in the guise of professionalism is downright criminal. It unduly burdens you with unnecessarily getting the seller's consent for something. Do not agree to this.

How Long an Escrow?

Get plenty of time in the escrow to do the things you have to do before you become responsible for the day-to-day costs of your new home. If you have to have time to sell your house, move, take a vacation, gather more money, etc., demand a long escrow! Also, if you anticipate the new house being vacated early and plan to do some remodeling or redecorating get some wording like this in your first low offer: "Buyer intends to remodel/redecorate portions of the house, and seller hereby grants buyer and/or his agents permission to enter onto the premises for such purpose. Seller may post a notice of nonresponsibility." (This latter right is the process whereby the seller is not compromised by any lien which might occur from any workman's claim against the buyer.)

Brokers shudder at this type of request, most likely because the one thing at stake for them is their commission, and entering onto the property could in the most extreme case result in a problem that could kill the sale. Brokers have even been known to tell a buyer that entering onto a property and doing work in advance of the close of an escrow is illegal. They are wrong. Naturally, you as the buyer would have to demonstrate your financial responsibility to the seller and obtain his permission. A partial release to him of some of your down payment might be required, but all of this is possible and certainly not illegal.

Thirty days is a short escrow, 90 days is a comfortable middle length, and 120 to 150 days is quite a long escrow. The latter is usually only requested to provide time for liquidating a former residence, for a major interstate move or some other such delay.

The Value of Some "Trading Points"

If you anticipate a particularly ticklish negotiation, one device in offering is to include one or more elements in the first low offer that you do not even care if you get but that you can trade away in the counteroffer stage. Labor unions utilize this device constantly; why shouldn't you? For example, part or all of the furnishings (excepting personal items, of course) might be asked for, particularly if the furnishings are not very valuable. Sometimes the landscaping is very extensive and is in movable pots, tubs, etc. Ask for these movable plants and baskets. Later, if you have to leave it out, it will look like a concession. You will experience no feeling of loss when you have to trade such things away.

Ask for a Preliminary Title Report

In your offer, request an inspection and approval of the preliminary title report. This will be sent to you from the escrow, a few days after opening. You should review it for any possible flaws or peculiarities in the title. Mainly, it reveals anything recorded in connection with the property loans, easements, rights of way, liens, quitclaim deeds, various notices, etc.

Unless there is something bad in the report, most states will not permit a buyer to use a disapproval of it to get out of an escrow. So don't plan to use it as a vehicle to exercise buyer's remorse, unless you are hunting for a law suit. Usually seven days is sufficient time to give approval after receipt of the report.

Selection of the Escrow Office

Brokers almost always have their favorite escrow company or escrow officer. However, it is your money being put up, and if your bank or savings and loan has an escrow department, why should you yield to the desires of the broker just because it feathers his nest? Small escrow companies and some large ones are reputed to bestow gifts on brokers that favor them with business. This is a form of payola that does not benefit you, the buyer, in the least. On the other hand, placing escrow business with your own bank, your own savings and loan or the institution being asked to increase its present loan on the property could have a helpful effect on your own financial program.

Don't Forget the Termite Report

Ask for a termite report if the printed escrow instructions of the escrow office do not include such wording. It goes like this:

"The Seller agrees at his expense to furnish Buyer in escrow with a current report in writing of an inspection by a licensed structural pest control operator of the buildings located at_____."

How Large a Deposit Check Should Accompany Your Offer?

Some brokerage firms have a policy of requiring 10 percent as a deposit check to accompany the offer. This is an outmoded idea that is carried on only because this is required in probate sales. Any deposit check over $5,000 is a form of showing off. In fact, most offers, even on very large properties, are usually made with checks of $1,000 or $2,000, although more funds will later go into the deposit amount in the escrow if the offer is accepted.

24
FINANCING– THE ALL-IMPORTANT QUESTION

In evaluating a property with great potential for appreciation, whether it be a condominium or house, it is often wiser to consult the methods of financing than the price. This is emphasized in the expression, "Value remains long after price is forgotten." By looking above your price range and exploring the various means of financing that might be open to you, an aggressive reach for just the right property will place you in the position of paying it off with cheaper and cheaper dollars and with deductible interest and property taxes. Thus, the old expression might be paraphrased this way: "Appreciation continues long after good financing has helped you forget the price."

First Choice in Financing: Having the Seller Carry the Paper

If, as is sometimes the case, the property under consideration is free and clear of any encumbrance, explore the idea of the owner carrying the financing on it himself. While most sellers do not want to commit themselves for a twenty-five- or thirty-year period for the note and first trust deed you would be giving him, an owner will occasionally go along with a ten- or fifteen-year note whose monthly payments are the same as if the note were of longer term, but with a "balloon" payment at the end of the tenth or fifteenth year. There are numerous advantages to this type of loan:

—It is not customary for the owner to charge any points or loan fee.

—The interest rate can often be set at a little less than you would have to pay for a maximum loan at a savings and loan.

—There would normally be no payoff penalty in the event you wanted to pay the loan off and refinance.

One unfavorable feature that can creep into the owner-financing picture is an "alienation" or "acceleration" clause—that is, wording that would require you to pay off the loan in the event you sold the property. Try to avoid this. If nothing is stated to the contrary, the note and first trust deed "go with the property," and when you resell the home, the loan can be assumed by the new buyer without any approvals being required.

Also try to avoid the requirement that you receive the owner's permission in order to pay off the note, much as we discussed in connection with the second trust deed.

Second Choice: Assuming the Existing Loan and Having the Seller Carry a Second Trust Deed and Note

The next best condition available is on houses that are already encumbered with a first trust deed from an institutional lender. The least costly maneuver is to apply to the lender to assume the existing financing with a minimum of disturbance, leaving the face amount of the loan the same. Without increasing financing, this often leaves a sizable gap between the down payment you can afford and the present loan. If the owner will carry a note and second trust deed that will help bridge that gap. Remember these desirable conditions:

—The note should have a minimum term of 5 years.

—The note should not contain an alienation or acceleration clause.

—The note should not bear interest higher than the first note.

—You should be able to pay the note off *at your option* without penalty. (To achieve this condition, the note will contain an "or more" clause.)

—Try for the concession of paying "interest only" for the first year, with principal payments to start at that time.

Third Choice—A Conventional Institutional Loan

The most common real estate loan is that made by the state and federally chartered savings and loans, and also some banks. The cheapest financing is from the seller, but next best is the maximum institutional loan available. If there is an existing loan on the property, there are some basic things you will need to find out about it.

—Can it be increased based on the sale price?

—What is the fee for the increase?

—What is the cost of transferring the loan?

—What is the cost of paying the loan off (the prepayment penalty)?

—Will the interest and payments remain the same after you assume the loan, or will there be an increase?

Often the cost of paying a loan off makes it mandatory that you continue on with the same lender, placing you at a great negotiating disadvantage in obtaining an increase in loan amount or holding onto a loan at existing rates of interest (if there has been a national upsurge in such rates).

There are a few trading points, though. If the lender wants larger monthly payments as a result of increasing a loan and upping the interest rates, request an extension of the overall term in order to pull those monthly payments back down. This adjustment may cost you 1 or 1-1/2 points but will leave you with a more comfortable monthly payment.

When it comes to the actual request to increase the loan, bear in mind that the lender works to a set formula in making maximum commitments. He will usually lend 80 percent of the first $40,000 of the appraised value of the property (generally the sales price will be accepted as the appraised value, *but not always*), and 70 percent of anything above that.

Therefore, you can see that if you are trying to minimize your down payment, you will either be driven back into the arms of the seller for a second trust deed or be totally dependent on the lender to extend the maximum amount he can.

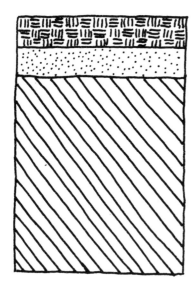

10%–15% CASH DOWN PAYMENT

10%–15% 2nd TRUST DEED

80%–70% 1st TRUST DEED

In times of high interest rates, the transfer of a loan is an irresistible opportunity for the lender to pounce on the buyer and squeeze his interest upward. Most loan agreements read in the small print that if the property is sold, the lender has the right to demand payment of his loan in full (the dreaded "alienation" clause). In effect his threat says, "Okay, if your buyer won't pay more interest, I will not approve the transfer of the loan, and you must pay it off entirely."

This condition has driven imaginative negotiators into a variety of ruses to hamstring the lender's avariciousness. A few are as follows:

—The *land contract* is where the title does not pass but only a *contract of sale* is entered into, with the "buyer" making payments to the seller and he, in turn, to the lender.

—The *all-inclusive trust deed* is a sophisticated invention where a new lender makes a bigger, all-encompassing loan but does not pay off the original first; he is actually only lending the *difference*. He receives payments from the buyer and transmits that portion due on to the first original lender.

—The *perpetual escrow* is a device in which title again does not change but where all necessary documents pertinent to a sale have been signed and deposited by seller and buyer in a perpetual escrow—and the buyer becomes a "person making payments." This goes on indefinitely until, theoretically, the entire loan is paid off, at which time title can be transferred to the buyer.

These examples are meant to underscore the sensitivity of the loan negotiation and the importance and difficulty of obtaining good terms.

Financing with Your Bank

If a property is free and clear or encumbered only by a small loan that would not be expensive to pay off, consideration should be given to financing with your own bank. A bank will usually not go quite as high on total loan amount as the savings and loans, but there are offsetting advantages here. Banks usually do not try to draw the last ounce of blood. Interest rates might be slightly less than the savings and loans. The initial point charge might be less, and payoff penalties will be more reasonable. All of these features would be beneficial if interest rates were expected to decline and you could arrange the bank loan to tide you over until such time as permanent long-term financing could be arranged at lower interest rates.

Insurance Company Financing—For the Borrower with a Special Need

Some very attractive real estate loan programs are available from major insurance companies. Their commitments are generous, their interest rates very fair, and loan charges and points well under what the savings and loans charge. However, there is one hooker. They will invariably tie in a life-insurance program with the real estate loan. Unless you have a *need* for life insurance, the net cost to you will probably be no less than other institutional financing when you consider the insurance premiums.

Home-Improvement Loans—More for Remodeling and Redecorating

This is a special loan made available at all banks and guaranteed by the federal government. Its maximum amount is $7,000. There is considerable red tape to processing one of these loans, and since it goes in a secondary position to the first trust deed, and since disbursement is made during the course of the remodeling project, there is no urgency to getting it processed at the close of your escrow. Information about this kind of loan can be obtained at your local bank.

An FHA Mortgage

This term refers more properly to government (FHA) mortgage insurance. It is significant to lenders in making loans on homes where very small down payments are involved. Regulations are quite strict regarding the type of construction, and there is a comprehensive manual of restrictions and approved materials and techniques.

FHA mortgage insurance costs 1/2 percent more than the going rate of interest, which premium is for the protection afforded the lender and is the amount charged by the government for the insurance. This additional cost is passed onto the homeowner-borrower in the form of slightly higher monthly payments. The advantage here is, of course, the smallness of the down payment, which can be as low as 5 percent.

One Word about Processing a Loan Application

One of the most vital parts of your loan application will be the statement of your financial qualifications. Do not be conservative and understate the various items. Be sure to show any stocks and real estate at *current market value,* not just what you paid for them, or even what you could sell them for in a hurry. The same goes for other real estate holdings. No one is asking you to sacrifice any of your assets, so it is perfectly proper to state them at values which are optimum.

25

THE ESCROW CLOSING...
AND MOVING IN

The Escrow Charges and Who Pays Them

The principal charges made for an escrow, exclusive of the cost of the house, are as follows:

	CHARGED TO SELLER	CHARGED TO BUYER
Escrow fee	1/2	1/2
Policy of title insurance	All	
Drawing deed		All
Stamps for documents		All
Recording new deed		All

Also, there are debits and credits for any taxes, bonds, rents, assessments, etc., that have been paid in advance or are owing by the seller. Since taxes are the largest figure and usually have already been paid, you must be prepared to budget sufficient funds for the portion of *prepaid taxes* you will be enjoying. Along this line, it is a good idea to call a week or so before the expected close of escrow and ask the escrow officer for the "estimated closing costs." The escrow officer can project the various charges and prorations, add them to your required additional down payment, and give you a fairly accurate figure. This way you will not be jarred by an unexpectedly high cash requirement if, say, the seller has paid his full year's taxes in advance, resulting in quite a heavy proration of monies to have to reimburse him.

Do remember that personal checks written to an escrow take several days to clear. Checks within the United States but outside of your own locale can take over a week to clear, and checks on foreign banks (including Canada) can take a minimum of two to three weeks to clear. If you are working close to the deadline, it is often necessary to provide the escrow with a cashier's check or a certified check from your bank so the escrow can close on time. Recording at the title company is usually scheduled for first thing in the morning on the day of closing, at 8:00 A.M. So do not count on anything else happening that day *but* the recording. All money matters will need to be completed well before that date of actual closing.

The Role of the Title Company in Conveying Real Property

In 90 percent of the states, *title companies* are enfranchised to issue policies of title insurance. In the remaining states, title is researched by an attorney who prepares an abstract of title. Each state differs somewhat in its method of conveying title to real property. The safest procedure, when in doubt, is to contact the state capital and inquire as to the statute or regulation concerning the conveyance of real property. This will set forth what procedures are required, what documentation, and what agencies, such as title companies, independent escrow companies, etc., are involved.

While the use of an attorney is recommended in any complicated transaction, and while it is mandatory in those few states that do not have procedures for issuring title insurance, in the majority of unsophisticated property transactions, an escrow officer or title company is capable of protecting the interest of buyer and seller and is, in fact, trained, licensed and normally bonded to do.

Extending the Escrow—A Touchy Subject

The escrow officer has some latitude in extending escrows beyond the agreed date of closing. However, the reason would have to be technical in nature and not due simply to the tardiness or omission by the principals. Therefore, if any delay in closing is desired, the matter should be discussed between the parties, their brokers, possibly their attorneys, and a proper escrow amendment drawn up and formally executed. Otherwise, you could be liable for a legal action due to a delay caused by yourself.

Brokers and Extensions of Escrows

Even though the buyer and seller may agree to an extension of the escrow, the broker should be consulted in this as well, for his job (for which he is to receive a commission) has technically been completed when he brings the buyer and seller together, and they have executed the deposit receipt and/or the escrow instructions. With his duties seeming to him complete, any delay after the time when he has a right to expect his commission should have his approval.

No fair-minded broker would oppose a legitimate delay, but if he feels put upon and wants his commission on time, a very reasonable gesture, particularly on a long delay of sixty days or more, would be to offer a release to him of a portion of his commission, say 25 to 33-1/3 percent. This would certainly be an expression of good faith. In the face of such an offering, the broker would have to be a real Simon Legree to refuse to co-operate.

The Status of the Termite Report as Escrow Closing Nears

The first knowledge of the results of a termite report often reveals two categories of trouble. First, there is the type of remedial work necessary to render the house free from termites and infestation that may presently exist. The cost of this work is assumed by the seller. This is usually covered by wording in the pest-control agreement like this:

"If infestation is found, Seller agrees to assume the cost for such remedial work as may be required or agree to the crediting of Buyer's escrow account to the amount of the necessary repairs, *at the election of the Buyer.*" The reason that this latter phrasing is a good idea is that if remedial work is to run, say, $300 to replace some old wooden porch steps and railings, plus part of the porch, this porch might be something the buyer intends to remodel, or perhaps to tear it out. If he holds the option of saying whether the work needs to be undertaken or not, he will be $300 to the good that he can then apply to the remodeling project rather than wasting it on old wood.

The second type of infestation reporting has to do with *preventive* work—such things as building concrete flash walls where the dirt of a planter comes up against wood siding, spraying attics, providing underhouse or attic vents, replacing old roof flashings, etc. This type of work is not the responsibility of the seller and is strictly in the province of the buyer.

As Escrow Closing Day Nears: "Look Around You!"

Be alert to any lack of progress of any work that is to be done on the house by the seller. Drive by the house a week to ten days prior to the expected closing date.

> Has the termite work been done?
>
> Is there evidence of any illegal removals?
>
> Does the garage look like it's about to become a dump yard?

Does it look like preparations for moving are taking
place?

Has any special cleaning effort been made?

It is discouraging, to say the least, to be the victim of an
eleventh-hour house move-out, where every trash barrel has been
filled to overflowing, the garage left glutted with cast-off clothing,
toys, broken furniture with notes attached to the Goodwill (who
do not even make their pickup until after the date you expect to
move in). How depressing it is to see cleaning people, or worse yet,
the owner's wife and children, ineptly struggling in a frenzy to
clean an entire house with too little time in which to do it.

Seriously regard the approaching deadlines, and if things appear
to be falling behind, nudge your broker into doing something
about it. People simply do not comprehend the time that packing
and moving and cleaning consume. Try not to be victimized by the
well-intentioned but naive seller. Push the panic button early, not
after it is too late. Motivate your broker to get the message across
firmly to the seller that you want maximum, not minimum,
cooperation. Have him make it clear that you do not want any
last-minute hurrying or lack of preparedness to mar your enjoyment of taking possession of the house.

The seller will be wanting to get his hands on your money, you
may be sure. He should be made to feel responsible for the
obligation he surely has to deliver the house and grounds in good
order at the appointed time.

Delays by the Lender—Getting the "Demand"

The escrow officer should make you aware of the progress of
any lending technicalities. Any delays in normal handling and
movement of papers should be followed up by your broker to
insure efficient processing of your loan. One feature, in particular,
can be troublesome, and that is the request by escrow for a
"demand." This is a written statement from any lender who is

about to be paid off showing the exact amount of all monies owed him including principal and interest up to the projected date of closing.

The escrow officer cannot, understandably, process this request for a demand too early because of the likelihood of a change in the actual closing date and the uncertainty about what interim payments have been made and in what amounts. Normally, a week or so before closing the request for a demand goes out. When the demand is received back, it constitutes the official authorization to pay off that obligation from the new loan's cash proceeds. Sometimes a note is held by a private party. What if that good citizen is traveling abroad? Ill? Inefficient in correspondence? Has to show everything to his "tax man?" Or to his attorney? What if those worthies are slow in reviewing it?

You can perceive the sensitivity of this demand procedure when everything is all ready to close and the possibility of delay looms. You or your broker should be closely clued into the mechanics of the demand as the closing of escrow nears. The broker might offer to "hand carry" a copy of any demand request to a private party, just to insure its safe arrival and improve the prospect for a quick response.

Insurance—Several Alternatives

Insurance instructions should be given the escrow officer at the opening of escrow. Three choices usually present themselves.

Continuing the existing insurance.

Canceling the existing insurance and having your own agent place your coverage on the property.

Yielding to the lender's request (frequently made) to let his own pet insurance company handle the coverage.

The second alternative is the best method of handling this. Many states make it illegal for the lender to require or even to imply that insurance should be carried by their pet insurance company—frequently a wholly owned subsidiary. Do not be cowed by the lender's insurance overtures; there is little danger of losing a loan commitment by balking at their salesmanship. In obtaining your own policy with your own broker and the companies he represents, you can better tie that policy into your overall insurance program—and maybe accomplish this with less cost and inconvenience. Also, your own agent will be benefited by the transaction, not some faceless employee of the house agency of your lender.

Adage: Trust Nobody!

Remember: Do not assume that everything is going along correctly at the house and in the escrow. Assume the worst, and you will not be disappointed. Visit the house and assure yourself that sufficient progress has been made in any cleaning or remedial work. The same goes for the escrow. Do not be afraid to ask the question, "What is still needed to close the escrow and what is the timing of those missing items?"

People working in calm office conditions day in and day out become accustomed to a certain controlled pace: phone calls, in-and-out stacks of mail, coffee, and much routine. When conditions seem hectic and filled with tension, those events are often very tame compared with the realities of the robust, free-lance world. You are putting up a sizable amount of money, your broker is willing (hopefully) to run all over the country carrying papers and getting signatures, your family is panting to move in, the lender is being cozy about releasing paperwork, the seller appears to be doing nothing about getting ready to move . . . *these are realities!* Do not be daunted by the seeming office-armor of escrow clerks and savings and loan secretaries. Push through their defensive veneer. Get your show on the road! Ask pertinent questions and make reasonable but firm demands. It will pay off.

Utilities—What to Do about Them

Caution your broker or the seller's broker not to permit any utilities to be turned off. These should simply be transferred to your name at the date of closing. Often the utility company is not notified until after the closing date, and this, of course, makes prorations of charges difficult and quite arbitrary if a meter has to be read.

Electricity   Water
Gas   Telephone
TV cable service

These are the agencies to notify. See that this is done well in advance, and you will be assured that a correct division of costs is made.

Cleaning the House

Nothing, repeat, nothing is more aggravating than receiving a house on the date of closing that has been inadequately cleaned. This situation is particularly irksome in the case of a sale where no redecorating or remodeling is to be done, where you intend to commence living in the house immediately.

The subject of cleaning should be initiated somewhere in the negotiation stage and an understanding reached as to the method and timeliness. It seems odd that a landlord holds a cleaning deposit on the most modest apartment, and on an expensive one up to $500, and yet something as costly as a house changes hands without some monetary assurance that the cleaning will be done. Since the change in ownership of a home is a much more important transfer, there is no reason why this cleaning feature should have less importance than any other. Somehow it gets lost in the shuffle, until the buyer sadly realizes that he has been delivered a filthy house and has no recourse. The control of $200 or $300 held in escrow until you give a release would permit you to have the cleaning work done by professionals if necessary, so your takeover would begin auspiciously with an immaculate home.

Moving In

Do: Get boxes in advance.

Prepare in advance.

Mark contents on the boxes (in case some are not to be unpacked right away).

Use the move as an opportunity to discard unwanted furniture, clothes and belongings.

Disconnect appliances in advance and schedule their connection in advance.

Don't: Plan on anything else on moving day.

Leave your spouse with the whole problem and both ends of the move to worry about.

Try to do it all yourself. Use professionals.

The first moment that you stand in the newly vacated house may be a depressing one, for all is bare, unoccupied, unhumanized. Just think ahead to the pleasurable moments of placing your own belongings in these new spaces, buying new things, cherishing old ones. You and your family will be giving it a new soul. You have this to look forward to.

APPENDIX A

Following is a partial list of requirements on Linda Isle:

1. Architectural approval by a committee of residents and the original developer required for all new construction and alteration of existing structures. This includes outside painting and decorating.

2. Minimum two-car garages to be enclosed: *No car ports!* In addition, electric garage-door operators are required.

3. Windows and door openings must be uniformly trimmed or uniformly recessed—that is, not just nailed on in the same flat plane with the stucco or siding. (This results in a designed, textural look, and tends to break up long, flat wall surfaces.)

TRACT HOME   CUSTOM HOME

4. Specimen trees are required to be planted with new construction along with other plants, shrubs, lawns, and sprinkler systems.

5. Proper drainage is required (so that water neither drains onto another's property nor stands on your own).

6. All wrought-iron railings must be galvanized or metalized to protect against future rusting. Also, stains are recommended on wood surfaces as opposed to paints in order to reduce the maintenance problem.

7. Roof design shall have a minimum pitch of 3 feet up for every running 12 feet to a maximum of 9 feet up for every 12:

8. Television antennae must be concealed inside attic spaces and not exposed on roof; this also applies to FM antennae.

9. No separate mail boxes are allowed; either boxes or slots must be built into exterior garage or house walls.

This still leaves plenty of latitude in which the skilled designer or architect can work. What it *does* do is remove the danger that a willful and sometimes spiteful eccentric will erect a huge ham radio tower on top of his house, or paint his shutters red, or cover his home with pink asbestos shingles. Therefore, do not react negatively if there are restrictions on new and remodeled houses in your proposed location. They are intended to preserve your property values and are one of your main buttresses in looking forward to a gain in the value of your home.

APPENDIX B

Monthly Payment Based on 25-Year Loan

Amount	Interest:				
	6%	6.6%	7%	7.5%	8%
$15,000	96.55	102.30	106.10	110.90	115.80
20,000	128.27	136.30	141.40	147.80	154.44
25,000	161.10	170.40	176.70	184.80	193.00
30,000	193.30	204.50	212.10	221.70	231.60
35,000	225.60	238.60	247.40	258.70	270.20
40,000	257.80	272.60	282.80	295.60	308.88
45,000	290.00	306.70	318.10	332.60	347.40
50,000	322.22	340.80	353.40	369.50	386.00
55,000	354.40	374.90	388.88	406.50	424.50
60,000	386.60	408.90	424.10	443.40	463.11
65,000	418.88	443.00	459.50	480.40	501.70
70,000	451.11	477.10	494.80	517.30	540.30
75,000	483.33	511.20	530.10	554.30	578.90

INDEX

HOME BUYER'S NOTES

HOME BUYER'S NOTES

HOME BUYER'S NOTES

HOME BUYER'S NOTES

HOME BUYER'S NOTES

HOME BUYER'S NOTES

HOME BUYER'S NOTES

HOME BUYER'S NOTES

HOME BUYER'S NOTES

HOME BUYER'S NOTES

HOME BUYER'S NOTES